THE CHINA SYNDROME

THE CHINA SYNDROME

Grappling with an Uneasy Relationship

Harsh V. Pant

HarperCollins *Publishers* India
a joint venture with

New Delhi

First published in India in 2010 by
HarperCollins *Publishers* India
a joint venture with
The India Today Group

Copyright © Harsh V. Pant 2010

ISBN: 978-81-7223-924-4

2 4 6 8 10 9 7 5 3 1

Harsh V. Pant asserts the moral right to be identified as
the author of this work.

The views and opinions expressed in this book are the author's own and
the facts are as reported by him which have been verified to the extent
possible, and the publishers are not in any way liable for the same.

All rights reserved. No part of this publication may be reproduced,
stored in a retrieval system, or transmitted, in any form or by any means,
electronic, mechanical, photocopying, recording or otherwise,
without the prior permission of the publishers.

HarperCollins *Publishers*
A-53, Sector 57, Noida 201301, India
77-85 Fulham Palace Road, London W6 8JB, United Kingdom
Hazelton Lanes, 55 Avenue Road, Suite 2900, Toronto, Ontario M5R 3L2
and 1995 Markham Road, Scarborough, Ontario M1B 5M8, Canada
25 Ryde Road, Pymble, Sydney, NSW 2073, Australia
31 View Road, Glenfield, Auckland 10, New Zealand
10 East 53rd Street, New York NY 10022, USA

Typeset in 11.5/14 Bembo Roman at
SÜRYA

Printed and bound at
Thomson Press (India) Ltd.

For
Ma and Babba

CONTENTS

Acknowledgements	ix
Preface	xi
1. Introduction	1
2. The Sino-Indian Convergence: Bilateral and Global	15
3. Diverging Trajectories	37
4. A Contrast in Global Profiles	72
5. India's China Problem: Why the Lack of a Serious Response	120
Epilogue	154
Notes	158
Index	178
About the Author	186

ACKNOWLEDGEMENTS

THOUGH ONE WRITES a book in the solitary confines of one's study, it is essentially a collective enterprise. It was only with the help, support and encouragement of a number of people that this project could come to fruition.

This book would not have been possible without the help and guidance I have received over the years from numerous scholars, thinkers and policy makers in India, who were willing to share their time and expertise with me. They talked candidly about their hopes and fears about China and in so doing helped me understand the complexities of Indian foreign policy making. There is no way I can acknowledge their contributions in these few words. But my heartfelt thanks to each and every one.

Krishan Chopra at HarperCollins India was very enthusiastic about this project at every stage and kept me going. A number of deadlines were missed but Krishan's understanding and support never wavered.

Finally, a special note of thanks to my family and my wife, Tuhina, in particular, who had to put up with my long absences from home. She did so with great patience and in so doing considerably lightened my task.

I dedicate this book to my parents who are just about the best parents a person could hope for. Thank you, Ma and Babba, for providing me with the secure and loving foundation from which to grow!

PREFACE

> Strategy without tactics is the slowest route to victory.
> Tactics without strategy is the noise before defeat.
>
> —Sun Tzu

ACCORDING TO MOST political observers, the global political architecture is undergoing a fundamental transformation with power increasingly shifting from the West to the East. The two most populous nations on the earth, China and India, are on their way to becoming economic powerhouses and are shedding their reticence in asserting their global profiles. Japan is gradually flexing its military muscle and the South-east Asian economies are back in business after the setbacks of the 1997 financial crisis. Whether it is such hopeful prospects or the challenges ahead in the Korean peninsula, Taiwan, and Kashmir, it is clear that this new century will, in all likelihood, be an Asian century.

The future of this Asian century will to a large extent depend upon the relationship between China and India. Their relationship will define the contours of the new international political architecture in Asia and the world at large. According to the United States National Intelligence Council Report titled 'Mapping the Global Future', by 2020, the international community will have to confront the military, political and economic dimensions of their rise. This report likened the emergence of China and India in the early twenty-first century to the rise of Germany in the nineteenth and America in the twentieth, with impacts potentially as dramatic.

The importance of their relationship is not lost on the two regional giants. In one of his meetings with the Indian prime minister, the Chinese premier, Wen Jiabao, is reported to have remarked: 'When we shake hands, the whole world will be watching.' As of today, however, the trajectory of the Sino-Indian relationship remains as hard as ever to decipher, despite some remarkable positive developments in the last few years.

This book attempts to explore this complex, multilayered relationship from the perspective of Indian foreign policy priorities. It focuses on the recent developments in the Sino-Indian relationship and argues that there does not seem to be any coherent long-term strategic vision in so far as India's China policy is concerned. After examining the recent convergence and divergence in Sino-Indian interests, it goes on to analyse the constraints that have made it difficult for Indian decision makers to carve out a coherent strategic approach towards China.

China's rise will be one of the most important forces shaping this century. And unless Indian foreign policy is able to come to grips with this reality, it will find it difficult to preserve and enhance Indian interests. Apart from constant media chatter about China, there is little serious attempt in the Indian political establishment, policy-making circles, academia and civil society to think through the implications of China's rise, perhaps the greatest geopolitical event of our times. While China has displayed a remarkable consistency in its dealings with India, India seems satisfied in muddling along from one high-level visit to another, anxious to keep China pleased at any cost. This lack of a guiding strategic framework in its China policy can have grave implications for India's national security interests as well as for its emergence as a global player of any reckoning.

The China Syndrome is an examination of the reasons for this lack of a strategic framework and the outcome in the form of a China policy that remains mired in confusion, contradictions, and clichés. It is not an academic treatise nor does it pretend to have any answers; it merely intends to be a polemic on the contemporary state of India's China policy, so as to encourage a broader debate on this crucial issue in the strategic community as well as the general public. If Indian policy makers are serious about India's global rise, this debate on China and India foreign policy is something that cannot be wished away.

1

INTRODUCTION

AS TENSIONS HAVE risen between India and China over the past few years, India has been awash with predictions about impending hostilities. Most recently, it has been suggested that China would attack India by 2012, primarily to divert attention from its growing domestic troubles. This suggestion received wide coverage in the media, which was more interested in sensationalizing the issue rather than interrogating the claims with the seriousness they deserved. Meanwhile, the official Chinese media picked up the story and gave it another spin. It argued that while a Chinese attack on India is highly unlikely, a conflict between the two neighbours can occur in one scenario: an aggressive Indian policy on the border dispute pushing China into using force. It went on to speculate that the 'China-will-attack-India' line might just be a pretext for India's deployment of more troops in the border areas.

This curious exchange reflects an undercurrent of

uneasiness that exists between the two neighbours as they continue their ascent in the global inter-state hierarchy. Even as they sign documents with high-sounding words year after year, the distrust between them is actually growing at an alarming rate. Paradoxically, economic cooperation and bilateral political as well as socio-cultural exchanges are at an all-time high. China is today India's largest trading partner. Yet, this has done little to assuage their concerns regarding each other's intentions. The two sides are locked in a classic security dilemma where any action taken by one is immediately interpreted by the other as a threat to its interests.

Global Coordination and Bilateral Tensions

At the global level, the rhetoric is all about cooperation, and indeed the two sides have worked together on climate change, trade negotiations as well as in demanding a restructuring of international financial institutions as the world economy's centre of gravity shifts. At the bilateral level, however, things came to such a pass that China took its territorial dispute with India all the way to the Asian Development Bank (ADB), where it blocked an application by India for a loan that included development projects in the north-eastern state of Arunachal Pradesh, which China continues to claim as part of its own territory. Buoyed by the perception that the Obama administration plans to make its ties with China the centerpiece of its foreign policy in the light of American economic dependence on it, China has displayed a distinctly aggressive stance towards India. The suggestion by the Chinese to the US Pacific Fleet commander that the Indian Ocean should be recognized as a Chinese sphere of influence has raised hackles in New Delhi. China's lack of support for the US-India civilian nuclear energy cooperation pact which it tried to block at the Nuclear Suppliers Group (NSG), and its obstructionist stance in bringing the terror masterminds of the 2008 November carnage in Mumbai to justice has further strained ties.

Sino-Indian frictions are growing and the potential for conflict remains high. Alarm is rising in India because of frequent and strident claims being made by China along the Line of Actual Control in Arunachal Pradesh and Sikkim, also in the north-east. China has upped the ante on the border issue. Indian has complained that there has been a dramatic rise in Chinese intrusions over the last two years, most of them along the border in regions of Arunachal Pradesh that China refers to as 'Southern Tibet'. China protested against the Indian prime minister's visit there in 2009, asserting its claims over the territory. But what has caught most observers of Sino-Indian ties by surprise is the vehemence with which Beijing has contested every single recent Indian administrative and political action in the state, even denying visas to Indian citizens of Arunachal Pradesh. The Indian foreign minister was forced to go on record that the Chinese army 'sometimes' does intrude on its territory, though he added that the issues were being addressed through established mechanisms. Boundary negotiations have been a disappointing failure with a perception in India that China is less than willing to adhere to earlier political understandings on how to address the dispute. Even the rhetoric has degenerated to an extent that a Chinese analyst connected to China's Ministry of National Defence could claim in an article that China could 'dismember the so-called "Indian Union" with one little move' into as many as thirty states.[1]

INDIA'S GROWING CHALLENGE

India's challenge remains formidable. It has not yet achieved the economic and political profile that China enjoys regionally and globally. But it gets increasingly bracketed with China as a rising power, emerging power or even a global superpower. Indian elites, who have been obsessed with Pakistan for the last six decades, suddenly have found a new object of fascination. India's main security concern now is not the increasingly decrepit state of Pakistan but an ever more assertive China, which is widely viewed in India as having a better ability for strategic planning. The defeat at the hands of the Chinese in 1962 has psychologically scarred the elite perceptions of China and they are unlikely to change in the near future. China is viewed by a large section of the Indian elite as an aggressive nationalistic power whose ambitions are likely to reshape the contours of the regional and global balance of power with deleterious consequences for Indian interests.

Indian policy makers, however, continue to believe

that Beijing is not a short-term threat to India but needs to be watched over the long term, though defence officials are increasingly warning in blunt terms about the disparity between the two. A former naval chief has said that the country neither has 'the capability nor the intention to match China force for force' in military terms, while a former air chief has suggested that China poses more of a threat to India than Pakistan.

It may well be that the hardening of the Chinese posture towards India is a function of its own sense of internal vulnerabilities, but that is hardly a consolation to Indian policy makers, who have to respond to a public opinion that increasingly wants their nation to assert itself in the region and beyond. India is rather belatedly gearing up to respond with its own diplomatic and military overtures, setting the stage for Sino-Indian strategic rivalry.

The rise of China is a major factor in the evolution of Indo-Japanese ties, as is the US attempt to build India into a major balancer in the region. Both India and Japan are well aware of China's not-so-subtle attempts at preventing their rise. It is most clearly reflected in China's opposition to the expansion of the United Nations (UN) Security Council to include India and Japan as permanent members. China's status as a permanent member of the Security Council and as a nuclear weapon state is something that it would be loathe to share with any other state in Asia. India's 'Look East' policy of active engagement with the Association of South East Asian Nations (ASEAN) and East Asia remains largely predicated upon Japanese support. India's participation in the East Asia Summit was facilitated by Japan, and the East Asia Community proposed by Japan to counter China's proposal of an East Asia Free Trade Area also includes India. While China has resisted the inclusion of India, Australia, and New Zealand in the ASEAN, Japan has strongly backed the entry of all three nations.

The convergence in the strategic priorities of India and the US as well as Japan notwithstanding, it is unlikely that India would openly become a part of the US-led alliance framework against China. Like most states in the Asia-Pacific, India would not want to antagonize China by ganging up against it.

Yet, India is the country that will be and already is being most affected by a rising China. As India comes into its own, as an economic and political power of global significance, ties between the two are at a critical juncture, with India trying to find the right policy mix to deal with its most important neighbour.

The Sino-Indian Security Dilemma

China has always viewed India as a mere regional player and has tried to confine India to the peripheries of global politics. It was being argued a few years ago that India was not on the radar of China: it had set its eyes much higher. Today, the rise of India poses a challenge to China in more ways than one – the most important being ideological. The success of the Indian developmental model poses a significant challenge for the Chinese regime. And as the story of India's success is being celebrated across the world, especially in the West, it is no surprise to see China becoming edgier in its relationship with India.

It is notable that only after the US started courting India did the Chinese rhetoric towards India undergo a slight modification. Realizing that a close US-India partnership would change the regional balance of power to its disadvantage, China has started tightening the screws on India. It has further entrenched itself in India's neighbourhood even as Sino-Indian competition for global energy resources has gained momentum. The development of infrastructure by China in its border regions with India has been so rapid and effective, and the Indian response so lackadaisical, that the member of Parliament from Arunachal Pradesh was forced to suggest that the government should allow Arunachal to get a rail link from China as even sixty years after independence India has failed to connect his state to the nation's mainland.

India, in response, is now trying to catch up with China by improving the infrastructure on its side of the border areas. It has deployed two additional army divisions and heavy tanks, and ramped up its air power in the region. Tensions are inherent in such an evolving strategic relationship, as was underlined in an incident in 2009, when an Indian Kilo-class submarine and Chinese warships, on their way to the Gulf of Aden to patrol the pirate-infested waters, reportedly engaged in rounds of manoeuvring as they tried to test for weaknesses in the others' sonar system. The Chinese media reported that the warships forced the Indian submarine to the surface, which was strongly denied by the Indian Navy.[2]

China and India are rising in an Asia-Pacific strategic landscape that is in flux. What is causing concern in Asia and beyond is the opacity that seems to surround China's military build-up, with an emerging consensus that Beijing's real military spending is at least double the announced figure. The official figures do not include the cost of new weapon purchases, research or other big-ticket items for China's highly secretive military. From Tokyo to New Delhi, from Jakarta to Canberra, there are calls for China to be more open about the intentions behind this dramatic pace of increase in expenditure and scope of its military capabilities.

Whatever Chinese intentions might be, consistent increases in defence budgets over the last several years have put the country on track to become a major military power and the one most capable of challenging American predominance in the Asia-Pacific. While China's near-term focus remains on preparations for potential problems in the Taiwan Straits, its nuclear force modernization, its growing arsenal of advanced missiles, and its development of space and cyberspace technologies are changing the military balance in Asia and beyond.

INDIA'S LACK OF LEVERAGE

A rising China will find it difficult to tolerate a rising India as its potential peer competitor. Even if India might be a long way off from challenging Chinese regional predominance, it is unlikely that China will leave anything to chance: it will try its best to contain

India, as it has already done to a large extent. And it is this containment that India will be forced to guard against. China's intentions towards India may seem entirely peaceful at the moment, but that is largely irrelevant in the strategic scheme of things. A troubled history coupled with the structural uncertainties engendered by their simultaneous rise is propelling the two countries into a trajectory that they might find rather difficult to navigate in the coming years. Notwithstanding notions such as 'Chindia' being romanticized in certain quarters, India cannot possibly allow China a free hand in shaping the strategic environment of the region.

The problem, however, is that India has no real bargaining leverage with China, and major power relationships are difficult to manage in the absence of leverage. Domestic political constraints in New Delhi and the lack of any incentive on the part of China has allowed the border problem to fester for far too long. India, moreover, is not making any serious effort to get economic, diplomatic or military leverage with its most powerful neighbour. It seems to have lost the argument over Tibet to China, despite the fact that Tibet constitutes China's only truly fundamental vulnerability with regard to India. India has failed to limit China's military use of Tibet despite its great implications for Indian security, even as Tibet has become a platform for the projection of Chinese military power. On its part, India has found it difficult to summon enough self-confidence to even allow peaceful protests by the Tibetans and forcefully condemn Chinese physical assaults on its Tibetan minority and verbal assaults on the Dalai Lama.

THE PAST AS PROLOGUE

As India embarks on redefining its foreign policy priorities to match its growing weight in the international system, it is imperative for its policy makers to learn from the nation's past so as to frame responsible policies for the future. The Central Intelligence Agency (CIA) of the US declassified its decades-old documents, referred to as 'family jewels', in 2007, which included its own assessment of the reasons behind India's debacle in the 1962 Sino-Indian war.[3] While we do not get any major new insight into the events from the assessment, it reinforces some of the issues that India can only ignore at its peril.

When the then Chinese president Liao Shao Chi said that 'China was a great power and had to punish India once' it was clear that India was being viewed as a threat in the long term and the 1962 war was as much about China's demonstration of its might as it was about the boundary dispute that apparently was the proximate cause behind the conflict. The Chinese military superiority in the 1950s, bolstered by India's own woolly eyed approach to security issues, provided China with a window of opportunity that it exploited to its advantage. The Chinese aim was not only to demolish Nehru's rising stature in the developing world but also to make sure that India's rise as challenger to Chinese primacy in the region was nipped in the bud. The CIA papers also point towards the use of Indian communists by China to portray Nehru as pro-America.

The CIA contends that '... Nehru himself refused to

change this policy [of gentlemanly persuasion] until long after Peking's basic hostility [made him] rethink his China policy ... In the context of the immediate situation on the border, where Chinese troops had occupied the Aksai Plain in Ladakh, this was not an answer at all but rather an implicit affirmation that India did not have the military capability to dislodge the Chinese.' While Nehru continued to see war as unnecessary, his tendency to project his own beliefs about statecraft onto his adversaries paved the way for a conflict the consequences of which India continues to come to terms with even after more than forty years.

The coverage of these declassified documents in the Indian media seemed to underline the apparent 'cunningness' of the Chinese and how they were able to deceive Nehru and India. The so-called Chinese 'betrayal' of Nehru is a lesson that the media and many others in India seem to have taken to heart. The argument has been made that the Chinese could not be trusted today because of their behaviour in the 1950s and the 1960s.

Yet, reading the documents and examining the Chinese behaviour closely one finds that it was no different than the behaviour of major powers across millennia. China was not betraying Nehru, it was simply looking after what it perceived to be its national interests and seeking aggrandizement of power and influence at the cost of India, its weaker neighbour and a possible challenger in the future. By 1958 even Nehru seemed to have disavowed his faith in the Panchsheel, the five principles of peaceful coexistence, and started considering China as unreliable. But his foreign policy still relied on mistaken assumptions, becoming divorced from the realities of power politics, and the consequences for India were catastrophic.

CHINA: BENEVOLENT OR MALEVOLENT?

Today, as China and India emerge as major powers in the global hierarchy, it is imperative that the Indian policy makers take due note of their nation's history. However, the real tragedy is that even today Indian foreign policy with regard to China remains mired in confusion, contradictions, and clichés. Leaving aside the question of the ability of Indian elites to think strategically on national security, in the case of India's China policy, one is not even sure if the Indian political and foreign policy establishment understands the basic forces that shape and configure global politics. India's inability, or rather unwillingness, to see the world as it is rather than as it should be has become the bane of its foreign policy. The pursuit of friendly relations with China seems to have become an end in itself when it should be a means towards achieving India's larger strategic objective of emerging as a major regional and global player. Diplomacy without an overarching conceptual framework of foreign policy often becomes a technical exercise in splitting differences, leading to what many might consider appeasement.

The policy towards China continues to be premised on the 'liberal fallacy' that strategic problems will inevitably produce satisfactory solutions merely because they are desirable and in the interest of all. India views stable Sino-Indian ties to be in the interest of both China and India. It is indeed in the interest of China to have good relations with India at least in the short term, when it wants to devote its energies to economic development. But its policy for the medium to long term is clear: establish its pre-eminence in Asia and contain India. There is no reason why India should allow China a free hand in shaping the strategic environment of the region.

There is nothing really sinister about China's attempts to expand its own influence and curtail India's. This is not much different than the stated US policy of preventing the rise of other powers that might threaten its position as a global hegemon. Just as the US is working towards achieving its strategic objective, China is pursuing its own strategic agenda.

There is also nothing extraordinarily benign in China's attempts to improve its bilateral relations with India in recent times. After cutting India down to size in various ways, it would not like to see India coming close to the US in order to contain China. In this geopolitical chessboard, while both the US and China are using India towards their own strategic ends, India has ended up primarily reacting to the actions of others. The primary reason for this is a lack of recognition of the forces that drive international politics in general and the lack of an attempt to come up with a coherent strategy towards China in particular.

While it is true that a rising China will not tolerate India as its peer competitor – even if India might not have any intention of becoming a regional hegemon, and will try its best to contain India, as it has already done to a large extent – contrary to what many might think, China is not a malevolent, sinister international entity out there to demolish India – it is a state which is simply pursuing its own strategic interests in a hard-headed fashion on its way to achieving the status of a great power. It is time for India to realize that its great power aspirations cannot be realized without a similar cold-blooded realistic assessment of its own strategic interests in an anarchic international system where there are no permanent friends or enemies, only permanent interests.

2

THE SINO-INDIAN CONVERGENCE: BILATERAL AND GLOBAL

BILATERAL RELATIONS BETWEEN India and the People's Republic of China (PRC) have indeed come a long way after they touched their nadir in the immediate aftermath of India's nuclear tests in May 1998. China had been singled out as the 'number one' security threat for India by India's defence minister just before the nuclear tests.[1] After the tests, the Indian prime minister wrote to the US president justifying the tests as a response to the threat posed by China.[2] Not surprisingly, China reacted strongly and diplomatic relations between the two countries plummeted to an all-time low.

However, some twelve years later, relations between the two countries, at least on the surface, seem to be on a much firmer footing as they have tried to reduce the prospect for rivalry and expand areas of cooperation. The visit of the Indian external affairs minister to China in 1999 marked the resumption of high-level dialogue and the two sides declared that they were not threats to each other. A bilateral security dialogue was also initiated that has helped the two countries in openly expressing and sharing their security concerns with each other. Both China and India continue to emphasize that neither side should let differences act as an impediment to the growth of functional cooperation between the two states. India and China also decided to expedite the process of demarcation of the Line of Actual Control (LAC) and the Joint Working Group (JWG) on the boundary question, set up in 1988, has been meeting regularly.[3] As a first step in this direction, the two countries exchanged border maps on the least controversial middle sector of the LAC. Both nations have finalized a set of political 'guiding principles' that will govern the parameters of the dispute settlement. China has expressed its desire to seek a 'fair' resolution to the vexed boundary issue on the basis of 'mutual accommodation, respect for history, and accommodation of reality'.[4]

DECLARATIONS ABOUND

Prime Minister Atal Bihari Vajpayee's visit to China in June 2003 was the first by an Indian premier in a decade. The joint declaration signed during this visit expressed the view that China was not a threat to India.[5] The two states appointed special representatives in order to impart momentum to border negotiations that have lasted now for more than twenty years, with the prime minister's principal secretary becoming India's political-level negotiator, replacing the India-China JWG. India and China also decided to hold their first joint naval and air exercises. More significantly, India acknowledged China's sovereignty over Tibet and pledged not to allow 'anti-China' political activities in India. On its part, China acknowledged India's 1975 annexation of the former monarchy of Sikkim by agreeing to open a trading post along the border with the former kingdom and later by rectifying its official maps to include Sikkim as part of India.[6] After being closed for sixty years, the Nathu La pass, a century-old trading post between Tibet and Sikkim, was reopened in 2006. High-level political interactions have continued unabated since then. The two states have set up institutionalized defence consultation mechanisms to reduce suspicions and identify areas of cooperation on security issues.

Soon after assuming office in 2004 the Manmohan Singh government too made it clear that it was for closer ties with China and would continue to work towards this end. Singh's first national security adviser, J.N. Dixit, wrote that 'the Congress will continue the process of normalizing, strengthening and expanding India's relations with China, which is the most important factor affecting Asian security and stability'.[7] In his first address to the nation, the prime minister also emphasized the carrying forward of the process of further development and diversification of Sino-Indian relations.[8]

When Singh visited China in 2008, the two states signed 'Shared Visions on the 21st century' to jointly promote the building of a 'harmonious world' underpinned by common economic prosperity and global peace. The 'Shared Vision' suggested that Sino-Indian ties would have a significant regional and global influence and the development of this relationship would have 'a positive influence on the future of the international system'. Both sides agreed to a set of political parameters and guiding principles as a basis to carve out a final settlement on the border. Subsequently, they have decided to elevate the boundary negotiations to the level of a strategic dialogue whereby 'the entire gamut of bilateral relations and regional and international issues of mutual interest' will be discussed. A hotline between the Indian prime minister and his Chinese counterpart has been set up as a means to remove misunderstanding and reduce tensions at the earliest.

Economic relations between the two have been expanding with China now India's largest trading partner. Sino-Indian trade is expected to cross the $60-billion mark soon.

THE GLOBAL STRUCTURAL IMPERATIVE

It is at the international level, however, that India and China have found some real convergence of interests. Both share similar concerns about the international dominance of the US, the threat of fundamentalist religious and ethnic movements in the form of terrorism, and the need to accord primacy to economic development. They have expressed concern about America's use of military power around the world and both were publicly opposed to the war in Iraq. This was merely a continuation of the desire of both states to oppose the US hyperpuissance ever since the end of the Cold War.

Both China and India, much like other major powers in the international system, favour a multipolar world order where US unipolarity remains constrained by the other 'poles' in the system. China and India zealously guard their national sovereignty and have been wary of US attempts to interfere in what they see as the domestic affairs of other states, be it Serbia, Kosovo or Iraq. Both took strong exception to the US air strikes on Iraq in 1998, the US-led air campaign against Yugoslavia in 1999, and more recently the US campaign against Saddam Hussein, arguing that these violated the sovereignty of these countries and undermined the authority of the UN system.[9] China and India share an interest in resisting interventionist foreign policy doctrines emanating from the West, particularly the US, and display 'conservative attitudes on the prerogatives of sovereignty'.[10]

China and India have coordinated their efforts on issues as wide-ranging as climate change, trade negotiations, energy security, and the global financial crisis. Both favour more democratic international economic regimes. It is being argued that the forces of globalization have led to a certain convergence of Sino-Indian interests in the economic realm, as the two nations become even more deeply engaged in the international trading economy and more integrated in global financial networks.[11] They have strongly resisted efforts by the US and other developed nations to link global trade to labour and environmental standards, realizing clearly that this would put them at a huge disadvantage in relation to the developed world, thereby hampering their drive towards economic development, their number one priority. Both have committed themselves to crafting joint Sino-Indian positions in the World Trade Organization (WTO) and global trade negotiations in the hope that this might provide them greater negotiating leverage over other developed states. They would like to see further liberalization of agricultural trade in the developed countries, tightening of the rules on anti-dumping measures and ensuring that non-trade related issues such as labour and environment are not allowed to come to the WTO. They have fought carbon emission caps proposed by the industrialized world and have resisted Western pressure to open their agricultural markets.

CLIMATE CHANGE POLICIES

Sino-Indian coordination on climate change, global trade negotiations and in demanding a restructuring of financial institutions in view of the world economy's shifting centre of gravity has had a significant impact on the course of international politics over the last few years. As the date neared for the UN climate treaty to be negotiated in Copenhagen in December 2009, the West, led by the US, and emerging powers such as

China and India, tried to bridge their differences on how to curb greenhouse gas emissions.

The US wanted developing countries such as India and China to agree to control the emissions being produced by their expanding economies, setting timebound targets to this effect. China and India argued that this would hurt their economic growth and wanted the industrialized world to curb its pollution as well as fund new technologies in the developing world by underlining that they had low emissions per capita. There was no appetite in Beijing and New Delhi to concede ground on this issue, with both finding it politically difficult to agree on binding targets.

For the Obama administration, on the other hand, it was important that China and India take some meaningful steps on climate if it was to have any hope of persuading the sceptics in the US Congress of its own domestic climate change agenda. Therefore, carbon reductions by India and China were a 'core part of these negotiations' for the US.[12]

Even as the West and China and India agreed on the need for an agreement at Copenhagen, the two emerging economies made it clear that they could not accept legally binding limits on carbon emissions. Though around 80 per cent of world growth in carbon emissions come from fast-growing economies like India and China, their governments argue that even if these economies continue to grow at current levels for the next decade or two, their per capita emissions would still be below those of the developed countries.

China and India together blocked a protocol that

called for a more ambitious climate target and mandatory greenhouse gas cuts from both industrialized and major emerging economies. They joined Brazil and South Africa in drawing up a basic draft for negotiating cuts in greenhouse gas emissions on the principle of differentiated responsibility.[13] As a result, the West found it difficult to get its way at Copenhagen.

There have been some attempts by the US Congress to impose tariffs on products from countries that do not undertake emission cuts targets. This has drawn a strong negative reaction in India and China, which view such tactics as non-tariff barriers. The move is largely viewed as a protectionist measure imposed by the developed world to shield its businesses from the costs of its national emissions targets. One of the major stumbling blocks in global negotiations on climate change has been the reluctance of the developed world to make adequate transfers of finance and enabling technology to the developing world, thereby helping it reduce emissions without incurring as many out-of-pocket costs. India and China have tried to seek a bilateral arrangement with the US on this issue with an understanding that this can serve as a model for an agreement between the developed and developing world. India and China are also likely to undertake joint collaboration on environmental regulation and management, something that is more doable than more high-profile gestures.

India has followed China in devising its own domestic climate change policies and towards this end, the two have been conducting regular dialogues to exchange views on their respective action plans. China has declared that it is pursuing its National Climate Change Programme, which includes mandatory targets for reducing energy intensity and discharge of major pollutants, as well as increasing forest coverage and share of renewable energy, during 2005-10. India followed suit by committing itself to a mandatory fuel efficiency cap to begin in 2011, a change in its energy matrix whereby renewable sources will account for 20 per cent of India's power usage by 2020, as well as announcing an ambitious solar energy plan.

GLOBAL TRADE DYNAMIC

The World Trade Report 2009 has suggested that trade is in grave danger of shrinking over the next few years. Given this bleak outlook a revival of the Doha round of trade talks can send the right kind of signals to various stakeholders in the global economy. The West as well as China and India have hinted that they are also ready to re-launch efforts to reach a new global trade deal under the Doha negotiations. The Doha talks had collapsed in 2008 after coming very close to an agreement primarily because of differences between Washington and emerging economies, led by India, over proposals to help farmers in poor nations. China teamed up with India to scuttle the Doha round. Because of their much greater economic power compared to the past, states like China and India now have much greater bargaining power. The West has serious differences with the developing countries on the level of protection that can be given to farmers as and when the global market for farm products is opened up.

The US has suggested that developing nations such as India need to provide greater market access for the talks to advance. India and China argue that they cannot compromise on food security and livelihood concerns even as the US and the European Union (EU) remain resistant to scaling down agricultural subsidies for fear of offending their domestic farm lobbies. It is possible that a bolstered, re-elected Indian government might be more willing and able to make unpopular concessions at home for the sake of collective economic gains that benefit the world while incurring the wrath of farmers, something that its predecessor could not afford to do with an election looming. But this can happen only if the developed world provides reciprocal concessions by phasing out its own agricultural subsidies, something that is highly unlikely in a climate of economic turmoil in the developed world.

Officially, neither the US nor India and China have provided any specific details about their plans to break the impasse over the agricultural sector that has been the bone of contention. Though the dismal state of the global economy and the need to revive global trade might be prompting the US as well as China and India to rethink their earlier strategies, the domestic political constraints remain as strong as ever.

The Energy Matrix

According to the authoritative World Energy Outlook 2009, global energy requirements could be 50 per cent higher in 2030 than today and China and India together would account for as much as 45 per cent of that increase.[14] Asia is emerging as a major factor in shaping the global energy trends. The world's fastest growth markets are in the Asia-Pacific nations, which require increasing and steady flow of energy to fuel them. Economic forecasters predict a crucial turning point in the 'comfortable world' to which the industrialized nations have become accustomed, and the security of energy supply lies at the apex of this turning point. The growth in new energy demand will drive market forces and energy costs, which might have an impact on the affluent living standards of the West. Around 75 per cent of the growth in the world's oil demand in recent years has come from Asia, and it is projected that the region will account for almost 50 per cent of this growth in the coming years.[15]

High rates of economic growth and rising per capita incomes, along with rapid urbanization and a concomitant increase in vehicles on the roads, are shaping this growing demand in Asia. Moreover, production prospects remain poor and demand management policies are weak. The demand for oil in Asia has been heavily subsidized by the governments, and price controls make oil products much cheaper than on the international markets. Policies that encourage energy efficiencies and support research in alternative fuels continue to be politically unsustainable. The widening gap between energy production and consumption in most major Asian states is a significant threat to the region's energy security.

The global energy environment is further strengthening

these trends. The global supply outlook is highly uncertain, with fears of worsening instability in the Middle East and other producers. Islamist extremism, continuing instability in Iraq, and Iran's intransigence on the nuclear issue has generated fears about the long-term reliability of these supply sources. Other major players in the energy market such as Russia and Venezuela are increasingly using energy resources as leverage in their foreign policies, making it difficult to predict their reliability as energy suppliers. The high price of oil, along with growing import dependence, is making emerging markets concerned about the prospects of their economic growth.

Some have argued that the world has entered an era of inflated energy prices that is producing a boom in innovations and a slowdown in consumption. This is a new age of oil in which the main problem is not beneath the surface but above it. More than 90 per cent of oil reserves are under the control of producing countries, many embracing a policy of resource nationalism. This is what will raise tensions between producing and consuming countries.[16] Oil prices have gone up substantially in recent times. It is hard to predict the trajectory of oil prices, but there is an emerging consensus that even if oil prices go down from their present height, they will not go down very far or for very long.[17] In the Asian geopolitical landscape, moreover, it is the rise of China that is also shaping the attitudes of other regional states towards energy resources.

All these factors have combined to make energy security the main driver of foreign policies of major states in Asia. The states in the region are increasingly focused on energy diplomacy, and new alliances are emerging with the aligning of strategic ties to energy needs. With the major Asian states pushing for supply-line diversification, regional rivalries are bound to escalate. Energy security is the new buzzword and is gradually becoming an important driver in the social, political, and foreign policy transformation of major states in Asia. Energy insecurity, with consequent economic stagnation, could be the catalyst to trigger internal social turmoil and political instability, thereby sharpening intrastate and inter-state fault lines.

It is against this complex strategic background that states such as China and India are trying to shape their own energy policies. Their approach towards their energy predicament remains rather traditional in so far as it is largely state-centric, supply-side biased, mainly reliant on oil, and tends to privilege self-sufficiency.[18] It is towards an aggressive pursuit of energy resources, particularly oil, across the globe that China and India seem to have focused their diplomatic energies in recent years, with some far-reaching implications.

For some time now a debate has been going on with respect to the consequences of the global pursuit of energy resources by emerging powers. This debate has been largely focused on China, with some claiming that China's hunger for energy will force it to pursue policies that could be destabilizing, while others argue that China's energy needs will integrate it even more into the international system.[19] India's pursuit of energy security also brings to the fore some of the same issues, and as both China and India try to gear their foreign policies to meet this challenge, the dynamic between them is bound to have consequences.

With an economy that is projected to grow at a rate of 7 to 8 per cent over the next two decades, meeting its rapidly increasing demand for energy is one of the biggest challenges facing India. A burgeoning population, coupled with economic growth and industrialization, has propelled India into becoming the sixth-largest energy consumer in the world, with the prospect of emerging as the fourth-largest consumer in the next four to five years.[20] Rising incomes in India, while generating prosperity, are pushing demand for energy resources even further. India is not only rated as one of the highest energy-intensive economies in the world – energy intensity being a measure of energy required by an economy to produce one unit of GDP growth – Indians also pay one of the highest prices for energy in purchasing power parity terms. India faces a growing imbalance between the demand for energy and its supply from indigenous sources, resulting in increased import dependence.

The fluctuations in global oil prices have been a worrying trend for India. It has been estimated that a sustained 5 per cent rise in the oil prices over a year could dampen India's GDP growth rate by 0.25 per cent and raise the inflation rate by 0.6 per cent.[21] India can only sustain its high rates of economic growth in the long term if it is successfully able to bridge the increasing demand-supply gap. According to the Integrated Energy Policy Report of the Indian Planning

Commission, India will have to quadruple its energy supply to sustain an 8 per cent rate of growth for the next twenty-five years, which calls for an energy regime that ensures supply, manages demand, and balances pricing to enable growth. The report goes on to recommend that India pursue all available fuel options and forms of energy.[22]

The Indian government has only recently woken up to the realization that it has already fallen behind other major players, especially China, in managing energy security. India is now trying to work at multiple levels by opening up the domestic energy market to multiple players, thereby making it more competitive; by adopting relatively rational principles for pricing; by establishing a credible energy pricing regulatory framework; by diversifying beyond oil to access alternative energy sources such as nuclear power and natural gas; and by increased focus on exploration activities within its borders.[23] India is trying to increase fuel efficiency by slashing state subsidies on all petroleum products. But this is a politically contentious policy issue, and subsidizing of household necessities is viewed as essential for supporting the poor in the country. India is also trying to put its emphasis on the import of natural gas. Various proposals are in the offing to import natural gas from Central Asia, the Middle East, and even from its neighbours such as Bangladesh. India is also trying to promote investment in the exploration and production of domestic oil and gas, and it has had some successes in that regard in the last few years.

But these attempts are aimed at the long-term management of the nation's energy security. India's greatest challenge as of now is to ensure successful diversification of sources for oil procurement to minimize possibilities of disruption in supplies. It is towards this end that India has devoted its diplomatic energies in the past few years as it encourages its public sector companies to acquire stakes in oil and gas fields abroad. India, like China, is reshaping its diplomacy to serve energy needs, because its booming economy also needs new supplies of oil to ensure its continued growth. The one reality that Indian diplomacy has to confront in its search for the nation's energy security is the presence of China almost everywhere and its relative success in achieving desirable outcomes.

Both China and India are feeling the pressure of diminishing oil discoveries and flat-lined oil production at a time when expansion of their domestic economies is leading to greater demand for energy. They have made energy the focal point of their diplomatic overtures to states far and wide. More significantly, faced with a market in which politics has an equal, if not greater, influence on price as economics, the two have also decided to coordinate their efforts to secure energy resources overseas. In essence, China and India plan to work together to secure energy resources without unnecessarily bidding up the price of those resources, thereby agreeing to a consumer's cartel representing 2.3 billion potential consumers. Together, their combined markets and purchasing power offer an extremely attractive partner to energy-producing states, especially the ones that face Western pressure over their human rights records or the nature of their political institutions.

It has been argued by many that cooperation between China and India on energy issues is the only way ahead if both states want to gain economies of scale and negotiation muscle. In many ways, they face similar constraints in achieving energy security and a coordinated approach would benefit them both. Competition only ends up driving up the costs of acquisition, thereby diminishing future returns. And there has been a recognition of this at the highest levels of government in both states.

China and India have signed a range of memoranda on energy cooperation that cover a full scope of areas, including upstream exploration and production, the refining and marketing of petroleum products and petrochemicals, the laying of national and transnational oil and gas pipelines, frontier and cutting-edge research and development, and the promotion of environment-friendly fuels.[24]

They have agreed to strengthen the exchange of information when bidding for oil resources in a third-party country in order to realize mutual benefit. China has pledged to promote cooperation with India in civil nuclear energy and to view this cooperation in the context of climate change and increasing non-polluting sources in the energy mix.[25] A former Indian petroleum minister, Mani Shankar Aiyar, made it clear that he thought that India and China joining hands to bid jointly for oil and gas assets under a 'monopsonistic' arrangement was much better than the two states competing in their quest for energy resources. He had even floated the idea of an Asian energy grid that might follow the trajectory of the European Coal and Steel Community, which grew into the EU. According to Aiyar, 'India and China don't have to go through fratricide in order to arrive at the conclusion that it is better to cooperate on energy security.'[26]

Two of the most talked-about ventures exemplifying Sino-Indian cooperation in this area have been investments by them in the exploration of hydrocarbon fields in Iran and Sudan. China and India hold a 50 per cent and 20 per cent stake respectively in the development and exploration of the Yadavaran field in Iran, while China's share is 40 per cent and India's 25 per cent in Sudan's Greater Nile Oil project. The proposal for a single transportation route for natural gas imports from Iran has also been floating around, with the promise of extending the India-Iran gas pipeline via Pakistan to China. In a first alliance of its kind between the Chinese and Indian state energy companies, a successful joint offer was made to buy Petro Canada's 38 per cent stake in Al Furat Production Company, Syria's largest oil producer, which is operated and majority owned by Royal Dutch Shell. This was followed by India's largest gas distributor, Gas Authority of India (GAIL), setting up a joint venture with Beijing Gas Group Company to distribute compressed natural gas (CNG) in Beijing. It has also signed a memorandum of understanding with the China National Offshore Oil Corporation (CNOOC) to develop offshore oil and gas projects in Indonesia and Australia. India and China had also come together to jointly bid for stakes in oil ventures in Colombia and Kazakhstan. China has sought close cooperation with India in its offshore and deep-sea oil exploration projects.

From Global to Bilateral

The attempt on the part of India and China in recent years has been to build their bilateral relationship on the basis of their larger world view of international politics. As they have found a distinct convergence of their interests on the world stage, they have used it to strengthen their bilateral relations. They have established and maintained regular reciprocal high-level visits between political leaders. There has been an attempt to improve trade relations and to compartmentalize intractable issues that make it difficult for their bilateral relationship to move forward. India has tried to move beyond the border dispute and engage China on a range of other fronts. The Indian political establishment remains highly impressed by the rise of China and the way it has managed the process. The Indian prime minister, Manmohan Singh, for example, found a speech delivered by the Chinese premier, Wen Jiabao, in Singapore so enlightening that he wanted it to become essential reading for all Indians.[27]

India and China have strengthened their bilateral relationship in areas as distinct as cultural and educational exchanges, military exchanges, and science and technology cooperation. In fact, the two nations are working towards raising the level of bilateral relationship with the hope of creating larger stakes in each other's economic future. Bilateral trade has recorded rapid growth and the two states are even evaluating the possibility of signing a comprehensive economic cooperation agreement and a free trade agreement, thereby building on strong complementarities between the two. Given the complementary nature of their economies and the size of their markets, this nascent Sino-Indian cooperation holds the potential to dramatically alter the world trade balance.

There is general recognition of a division of labour within the information technology (IT) sector, with China manufacturing chips and electronic components and India excelling in writing the software. Indian software companies are increasingly setting up shop in China, sensing great opportunities there.[28] It was former Chinese premier Zhu Rongji who suggested that the combination of Chinese hardware and Indian software would be irresistible to the global market.

In addition to IT trade and interactions, India facilitates China's economic development by exporting raw materials and semi-finished goods, as well as shipping Chinese cargo overseas. Chinese companies, for their part, have begun to tap India's ever-expanding consumer market by exporting electrical machinery, home appliances, consumer electronics, and mechanical goods. Both nations are looking beyond the existing trade and trying to identify new milestones that can help intensify their economic ties, including greater exchange in scientific research and technology.

They are also taking steps to upgrade their military-related cooperation, leading to greater understanding on the bilateral military front, something that would have been unthinkable just a few years ago. As a first step in this direction, the Chinese and Indian navies carried out joint search and rescue operations off the Shanghai coast in November 2003. Their militaries conducted joint anti-terror exercises in 2007, the first time that Indian soldiers set foot in China after 1962. These ties between the two armed forces were reinforced when China and India conducted a joint army training exercise, the 'Join Hands 2008', aimed at combating terrorism. High-level delegations from India have been visiting China and vice versa, including officials in charge of army deployment along the India–China border. Both states are also seeking to cooperate on the nuclear front, with China planning to import heavy water from India to be utilized in the pressurized heavy water reactors near Shanghai.[29]

Many observers have also detected a subtle shift in Beijing's stance on Pakistan with regard to India. China's 'neutral' position during the Kargil conflict and the intense Indo-Pak warlike crisis following the terrorist attack on Parliament in New Delhi in December 2001 is for many a reflection of China's sincerity in its attempts to improve its relations with India. China is also seen as playing a central role in encouraging Pakistan to negotiate with India by using its leverage with Pakistan.[30] In keeping with China's attempts to project itself as a responsible regional player, China is seen by some as supporting peace and anti-terrorist efforts in South Asia by cooperating with the US and India. It has been suggested that China's rapidly rising energy requirements are forcing it to push towards moderating its behaviour as stable Indo-Pak relations are important for China to secure supplies of oil from Pakistan.[31]

All this reflects on India continuing to build its relations with China on the convergence of interests that they have achieved in recent years. The Chinese ambassador to India suggested in early 2009 that Sino-Indian 'bilateral relations are in one of the best periods in history'.[32] India is celebrating 2010 as the 'Year of Friendship with China'. Yet, examining closely one finds that the Sino-Indian relationship has become a lopsided one where India is expected to keep China in good humour at all costs even while China can work without any apologies to restrict India's strategic space. Even while professing its noble intentions, Chinese actions have more often than not adversely affected India. And India has remained reluctant to speak openly about the growing problems in its relationship with China. The present 'stability' in Sino-Indian ties is more a function of India deciding to sidestep contentious issues and instead focusing on largely those areas where cooperation is easier to come by. While this may seem attractive in the near term, it will have grave consequences for India in the coming years as it continues its ascent in the global inter-state hierarchy. The divergence between China and India is real, it is growing and it needs to be acknowledged.

3

DIVERGING TRAJECTORIES

INDIA AND CHINA indeed seem to have achieved some degree of convergence in their interests in recent years and India has decided to build its relations with China on the basis of that convergence. Yet, the trajectory of Indian foreign policy seems to be giving an impression that this is being done by ignoring the enormous obstacles that confront this bilateral relationship. There has been a dominant tendency in the Indian foreign policy establishment to focus on the strengths of its bilateral relations with China while pretending that the problems confronting the relationship would somehow take care of themselves. And the challenges in the Sino-Indian relationship are by no means insignificant, nor will China take care of Indian interests. It is for India to recognize them for what they are and evolve a coherent strategy to tackle the challenges.

China's Political Trajectory

The number one priority for China's leadership today is economic growth and social stability. China underwent one of the most peaceful and orderly political transformations in its recent history when Hu Jintao became the Communist Party chief in 2002 and the President of China in 2003, replacing Jiang Zemin. Jinag Zemin also finally ceded effective control of the armed forces to Hu Jintao in September 2004, thereby putting Hu formally in command of all the vast party, government, and military bureaucracies that rule China and its 1.3 billion people. This was a generational shift in Chinese political structure and although important for the smooth working of the government, it did not produce any radical change in its foreign policy as the focus of the political leadership remained on maintaining the high rates of economic growth.

Hu Jintao is part of the fourth-generation leadership of the CCP and is a product of the 'evolutionary policies' of Deng Xiaoping that emphasize economic growth and orderly governance. Not surprisingly, therefore, he has made it amply clear that Western-style multi-party democracy is something that would not serve the Chinese people well, terming it a 'blind alley' for China.[1] Domestically, he has talked of evolving China into a 'harmonious society' while emphasizing China's 'peaceful rise' in the international arena. Hu has been looking closely at the country's growing wealth gap and the environmental costs of its long streak of rapid economic growth. He has also managed to keep a tight leash on media and has been reluctant to take any meaningful steps towards overhauling the one-party system.

The Chinese Communist Party (CCP) is nothing if not adaptive to changes. By moving away from Mao's utopian dogmatism to Deng's pragmatism, the CCP has ensured its longevity in China, defying predictions of its collapse for the last three decades and managing to tackle the problems confronting China rather skilfully. In recent years, it has successfully absorbed entrepreneurs, urban professionals and university students into an elite class that is invested in the political status quo. The CCP realizes that it can only survive if it keeps on adapting to the changing times. And so it is harnessing nationalism to justify its rule while at the same time effectively buying off intellectuals and the middle class, who fear disorder much more than they want political freedoms.[2] Ironically, it is economic prosperity that, while raising people's expectations and access to information, has helped the CCP forestall democracy.[3] By embracing market economics while preserving the party's monopoly on power and restricting political freedom, the communist leadership is propagating a version of 'authoritarian capitalism' that seems to be serving its interests well, at least in the short term. The CCP even managed to use the 2008 Olympics to mobilize popular enthusiasm and gain international prestige, as was done by other fascist and communist regimes in the past.

Despite the long-standing fantasy of the Western liberals that economic engagement would inevitably bring democratic reforms to China, free-market conditions have not led to political liberalization. The CCP has learnt its lessons well from the demise of the former Soviet Union and fall of communism in Eastern Europe. The central conclusion the CCP drew is that it must remain ideologically nimble while continuously trying to refurbish its organs, outreach, and message, and the need to keep improving living standards, retaining the control of the media and avoiding European-style social democracy.[4] Economic growth has strengthened the CCP's hold on power, allowing it to feed on the boom it has helped create. The Seventeenth Congress of the CCP, convened in 2007, made it clear that the party has no intention of ushering in serious political reform. The emphasis of the Congress was on 'scientific', inclusive and sustainable development, and the phrase 'scientific development' was enshrined into the party constitution.[5]

The Chinese public perception about their country is striking. Three in four Chinese think the world likes China, while 90 per cent believe that China's global influence is positive. They think twice as many people in the world like their country as actually do. Only 47 per cent of the people in twenty-three countries reportedly believe that the Chinese influence is positive.[6] This should not be surprising, given the tight control that the Chinese political leadership exerts over the media and information, but it creates complications in China's ties with other states as it enables the CCP to manipulate information to generate nationalistic hype, especially where it is targeted at countries like Japan,

India and the US. The decision of the Chinese authorities not to allow Google to legally operate an unfiltered search engine underscores the importance the political leadership gives to maintaining its iron grip over the flow of information.

The varied political arrangements in China and India make the relationship highly susceptible to mistrust and conflict. The democratic peace theory suggests that democracies rarely, if ever, go to war with each other, but a democracy existing side by side a communist regime makes for a potent mix. The regime in Beijing is extremely vulnerable to domestic pressures and so tends to use nationalism to divert public attention from domestic problems. It has used nationalism as an ideology to hold the country together. This means that in the event of an economic crisis, as happened in 2008-09, constraining its ability to satisfy people's economic demands, it will be tempted to rely more and more on targeting its external adversaries. And India, in many ways, presents an easy target.

The perceptual differences between the elites in India and China also present a worrisome picture of the future of Sino-Indian bilateral ties. The level of distrust of each other's intentions remains high among the elites in Beijing and New Delhi. Despite all the talk of Asian solidarity, cultural differences between the two states remain strong. Indian political elites find it difficult to trust Beijing after 1962, especially as the war came after attempts by Nehru to forge strong ties. The Chinese elites also distrust India, especially after recent attempts by New Delhi to forge strategic ties with Washington and Tokyo, though for a long time India was not a priority for Chinese foreign policy. At the popular level too, negative perceptions abound. An opinion poll of ordinary Chinese ranked India after the US as the country most likely to pose a security challenge to China in the next ten years.[7] As India's former ambassador to China, Nirupama Rao, has suggested, 'negative perceptions among the people on both sides about Sino-Indian bilateral relationship remain a significant challenge'.[8]

CHINA'S ECONOMIC TRAJECTORY

China has enjoyed average annual rates of real income growth of around 10 per cent in the last two decades of the twentieth century, something unprecedented historically. China overtook Germany to become the world's largest exporter in 2009 and its share of world exports jumped to almost 10 per cent, up from 3 per cent in 1999.[9] China's share of world trade has continued to rise despite the 2008-09 financial crisis and it is the world's largest recipient of foreign direct investment, absorbing more than US $90 billion worth of FDI in 2008. It has been estimated that by 2040 China's GDP will reach $123 trillion and it will account for 40 per cent of the world's output.[10] China has already overtaken Japan to become the world's second-largest economy this year and according to various estimates, the Chinese economy may surpass that of the US by 2027. It holds more than $1 trillion in US government debt, that is but half the foreign reserves generated by its huge trade surplus and investment flows. China's state-owned enterprises are buying companies, technologies and resources worldwide. China became the first major economy to recover from the global recession and played a leading role in pulling the rest of the world out of it.

China's focus will continue to be on maintaining its high rates of economic growth for now, even as some of the economic challenges it faces will become more acute. The increasing income disparities, restructuring of its state-owned enterprises and the problem of non-performing loans in its banks are just a few of the problems China's economy is likely to face. So far China has managed remarkably well.

Instead of trying to take a tip or two from China's management of its economy, many in India either envy China or try to dismiss its economic growth as a façade.[11] Consensus still eludes India as to the right route to economic development and modernization. This is as much due to the democratic institutional structure of Indian polity as to a certain lack of will in the top leadership. The inability of India to rectify its infrastructural bottlenecks and raise its research and development spending substantially will continue to hamper the growth of its economy.

Though India has achieved some remarkable growth rates in the last few years, indeed enjoying average annual rates of real income growth of 6 per cent in the last two decades of the twentieth century, it still lags far behind China and will need many more years to match its impressive economic performance. China has outperformed India in terms of growth, the education, health, and living standards of its population, and in integrating its economy with the global economy. In sectors where India and China compete with each other for export markets, such as textiles, China is far ahead even as Sino-Indian competition for third markets is bound to further intensify. China's GDP is four times that of India's. India accounts for less than 1 per cent of world trade in goods and services and has been unable to market itself as an attractive a destination for FDI as China. Meanwhile, investments by China account for merely 0.01 per cent of total foreign investment in India. China's annual trade with India is only a fraction of its trade with Europe, Japan and the US. Indian exports to China are primarily dominated by raw materials and iron ore. India's challenge is to match Chinese exports to India and diversify India's export basket.[12] A rising trade deficit that is in favour of China is problematic for India, as is the Indian failure to use its core competencies to enter the Chinese market.

Sino-Indian trade tensions have also risen, especially as the economic downturn that started in 2008 began to make its effect palpable in China and India. Economic nationalism is on the rise in China and the business environment is deteriorating, with China attempting to force foreign companies to hand over their intellectual property and other trademarks if they want to keep selling their goods in China.[13] As the two states compete across the globe for export markets, energy assets, and investment projects, some amount of competition is inevitable. This economic rivalry is likely to intensify as both intrude into each other's strengths, with China shifting its economy towards services and high-tech industries and India trying to rapidly expand its manufacturing base. India remains concerned about Chinese imports flooding Indian markets. It has accused Chinese companies of swamping its markets with low-quality products, even banning, albeit briefly, Chinese-made toys in early 2009 for safety reasons. It is also the largest initiator of anti-dumping investigations against China under the WTO.[14] In the words of the Indian commerce secretary, 'Cooperation hasn't really worked.'[15]

India remains reluctant to open its domestic industries that haven't faced foreign competition and remains ambivalent about allowing Chinese firms a level playing field. The Indian security establishment continues to view Chinese firms with suspicion and as potential security hazards given that the People's Liberation Army (PLA) holds a stake in a number of the companies. China has complained that its investments are subjected to rigorous security reviews and work visas for its executives are not swiftly processed. China has been vocal about its concerns about the investment climate in India for its companies though most FDI proposals from Chinese companies have managed to receive clearance from the Indian government in recent years.[16] There has been talk of a Sino-Indian Free Trade Agreement (FTA) for some time now, but it is not readily evident that it would be a good idea. Given China's management of its currency exchange rate, some see in the FTA a 'yuan trap'.[17] Though some argue that the long-term economic prospects of India are much better than

China's – and Chinese policy makers, under pressure from the US to revalue their currency, are worried about India's competitive advantage[18] – China remains the undisputed economic powerhouse of the moment driving the Asian and global economy, with India lagging somewhere behind. As long as India does not place its own economic house in order, it will remain a second-rate power even in Asia. And China will remain the Asian power that the world will look up to when trying to manage problems in the continent and beyond.

CHINA'S MILITARY MODERNIZATION

What should be equally, if not more, significant for India is the fact that China's economic transformation has given it the capability to emerge as a major military power, spending as much as $65 billion a year on its defence forces.[19] China's military may or may not be able to take on the US in the next few years but it will surely become the most dominant force in Asia. According to authoritative sources, China is set to overtake Japan in the next decade to become Asia's major regional military power.[20] The US involvement in the global war on terror has put the 'containment' of China on the backburner and China has seized on this much-needed space to strengthen its armed forces further.

China has imbibed the lessons of the recent US military undertakings such as the 1991 Gulf War, and the wars in Afghanistan and Iraq. These have spurred China's pursuit of the Revolution in Military Affairs

(RMA), manifesting itself in the buying and adoption of latest technologies and weapons systems (particularly from Russia) and concomitant changes in doctrine and organizational structures.[21] The PLA has been shedding its manpower since the late 1990s to save funds so as to be able to focus on high tech. One of the lessons China's military has seemingly learnt from recent wars is that technological sophistication is the sine qua non for effective military operations in the contemporary strategic environment. The world's biggest standing army has already been reduced to 2.3 million soldiers, with spending now focused on better training and advanced state-of-the-art weaponry. China intends to reach the strategic goal of building informationized armed forces and being capable of winning informationized wars by the mid-twenty-first century.

Despite a Western embargo on China with regard to the transfer of military technologies, China has been able to deftly use US corporations to garner dual-use technologies and employ these for its military upgradation.[22]

The Chinese government released its latest defence White Paper in 2009.[23] This was the sixth such policy document from Beijing, the last one having come out in 2006, and an attempt by the Chinese government to assuage the concerns around the world about its military capabilities. And this time the Chinese Ministry of National Defence held a press conference about it.

That's because China's arms build-up has generated apprehension worldwide. Its defence expenditure has increased by an average of about 15 per cent a year from

1990 to 2005. Yet, the declared military spending by China only represents about a third of its actual expense, if equipment purchases are taken into account. China's official military spending figures do not include spending on its space programme, strategic forces, foreign acquisitions, military-related research and development and paramilitary forces. The rest of the world is making a concerted bid to engage China on military issues so as to remove the veil of secrecy that surrounds its military plans and spending.

But while China's White Paper made it clear that moving from infantry to high-tech naval and aerial warfare is a major goal, and it does talk about China's plans to build new types of submarines, destroyers, frigates and aircraft, no mention was made of aircraft carriers or of nuclear-powered submarines equipped with ballistic missiles, both expected to be added in the next few years. The White Paper offered no budgetary specifics, thereby not improving the transparency about Chinese defence spending – the ostensible reason for the papers. China has begun construction of two medium-sized aircraft carriers, and with a refurbished 55,000-tonne Soviet-built Kuznetsov-class carrier, the *Varyag*, China will have three operational aircraft carriers in the next five to six years. This will have a profound impact on Beijing's regional power projection. In the first-ever deployment of Chinese warships in distant waters, its navy is working to combat Somalian piracy. China intends to further develop its capabilities to operate effectively in distant waters.

While not mentioning the US by name, China's

White Paper makes a comparison between the present superpower and the emerging one. In contrast to a unilateralist America that apparently seeks to enfeeble China 'by supporting diplomatic struggles with military means', China itself, according to the latest document, 'will never seek hegemony or engage in military expansion now or in the future, no matter how developed it becomes'. Interestingly, the paper underlined the Chinese unease about changing policies of the US in Asia suggesting that 'the US has increased its strategic attention to and input in the Asia-Pacific region, further consolidating its military alliances, adjusting its military deployment and enhancing its military capabilities'.[24]

Sun Tzu wrote that 'supreme excellence consists in breaking the enemy's resistance without fighting'. The PLA is committed to modernizing, expanding and deploying a sophisticated military capable of seriously challenging American power. And this it is doing by focusing on the US military's vulnerabilities, pursuing an asymmetric strategy aimed at battle-space denial. In addition to sustaining and modernizing its nuclear arsenal, China is investing in new technologies for cyber and space warfare, primarily to counter America's traditional advantages. It is challenging US military superiority in the Asia-Pacific region. This was underlined in the report on China's Strategic Modernization by the US Secretary of State's International Security Advisory Board, which suggested that the US needs new weapon systems, including missile defences, and other advanced military capabilities to deter and counter China's steady build-up of nuclear and conventional weapons.[25] China's space weaponization is aimed at levelling the playing field in the event of a conflict with the US by targeting America's fundamental vulnerability: its satellites and their related ground installations.[26]

Beijing has made clear its intention of focusing on the development of asymmetric capabilities that include electronic warfare, shaping the battle space with information dominance and using new technology not available to great powers that modernized earlier. China has been probing the computer networks of its adversaries for some time now, investing heavily in electronic countermeasures and envisaging concepts like 'computer network attack, computer network defence and computer network exploitation'.[27] Its industrial and defence espionage is aimed at obtaining advanced technology for economic and military modernization.

The penetration of China into the Indian intelligence apparatus is growing to the consternation of many.[28] The National Informatics Centre – India's premier science and technology institution which governs and hosts all government websites as well as computers of the Prime Minister's Office, the Ministry of External Affairs, several Indian embassies, the Bhabha Atomic Research Centre, and the Dalai Lama – was infected by GhostNet, a China-based cyber espionage network. Though this came to light in early 2009, it has been going on for the last several years.[29] China has been giving cyber warfare serious thought and has incorporated it into its military planning and strategy by encouraging civilian computer crackers to penetrate the networks of key political and military leaders in countries ranging from the US, Japan, Taiwan, to India and South Korea.[30]

As a consequence of its growing capabilities, China has started asserting its military profile more significantly than before. In 2009, Chinese vessels tackled Somali pirates in the Middle East, the first time Chinese vessels operated outside Asia. Beijing is also considering sending combat troops abroad in support of UN peacekeeping efforts. Chinese military officers are openly talking of building the world's strongest military and displacing the US as global hegemon, by means of a war if need be. This might be a bit premature at the moment as the US military still remains far more advanced than China's, which does not yet possess the capability to challenge the US far from Chinese shores. It is China's neighbours who should be worried, especially as the US starts to look more and more inwards.

China's sustained military build-up will continue over the next few years and this will pose a challenge to Indian military planners as the military's modernization programme is fast losing momentum. India needs to urgently review its defence preparedness vis-à-vis China. As the policy paralysis post-Mumbai has revealed, India seems to have lost even its conventional superiority over Pakistan. The real challenge for India, however, lies in China's rise as a military power. If the latest White Paper is any indication, China already views itself as a superpower-in-waiting. The Indian government owes it to the nation to set this imbalance right. The Indian Army is indeed revising its conventional war-fighting doctrine that is aimed at deterring as opposed to dissuading China.[31] But what this means in operational terms remains far from clear.

According to an estimate by the Indian government's own China Study Group, China now possesses the capability to move more than 10,000 troops to the Indian border in twenty to twenty-five days, compared to three to six months a decade back. This is possible because of China's efficient border management, and it has forced India into constructing roads on its side urgently.[32] By engaging in repeated, though controlled, provocations, the Chinese military is carefully probing how far it can push India. The new military restiveness on the Sino-Indian border does not bode well for India, as the military balance along the long and contested border is rapidly altering in Beijing's favour. It is not without reason that China has upgraded its military and civilian infrastructure in Xinjiang and Tibet. As a consequence, Tibet has become a militarized zone.

China's enhanced military prowess will lead, as is inevitable, to an assertion of its interests more forcefully, more often than not, adversely affecting Indian interests. As China becomes more reliant on imported oil for its industrial economy, it will develop and exercise military power projection capabilities to protect the shipping that transports oil from the Persian Gulf to it. The capability to project power would require access to advanced naval bases along the sea lanes of communication and forces capable of gaining and sustaining naval and air superiority.

China's Naval Expansion

The Chinese navy is aiming at a 'gradual extension of the strategic depth for offshore defensive operations and enhancing its capabilities in integrated maritime operations and nuclear counter-attacks'.[33] With the largest Asian fleet, greater operational confidence and a global presence, the Chinese navy is flexing its muscles and sending signals that it seeks to be a dominant power in the Asia-Pacific.

China's navy is now considered the third-largest in the world, behind only the US and Russia, and superior to the Indian Navy in both qualitative and quantitative terms.[34] Speculation is rife that Chinese shipbuilding and acquisition spree will result in the People's Liberation Army Navy (PLAN) having more ships than the US Navy some time in the next decade. The PLAN has traditionally been a coastal force and China has had a continental outlook to security. But with a rise in its economic might since the 1980s, Chinese interests have expanded and have acquired a maritime orientation with an intent to project power into the Indian Ocean. China is investing far greater resources in the modernization of its armed forces in general and its navy in particular than India seems either willing to undertake or capable of sustaining at present. Its increasingly sophisticated submarine fleet could eventually be one of the world's largest, and with a rapid accretion in its capabilities, including GPS-blocking technology, could, some suggest, have the capacity to challenge America.[35] Senior Chinese officials have indicated that China would be ready to build an aircraft carrier as it is considered indispensable to protecting Chinese interests in the oceans.[36] Such an intent to develop carrier capability marks a shift away from devoting the bulk of PLA's modernization drive to the goal of capturing Taiwan.

China is acquiring naval bases along the crucial choke points in the Indian Ocean not only to serve its economic interests but also to enhance its strategic presence in the region. There is enough evidence to suggest that China is comprehensively building up its maritime power in all dimensions.[37] Its growing reliance on bases across the Indian Ocean region is a response to its perceived vulnerability, given the logistical constraints that it faces due to the distance of the Indian Ocean waters from its own area of operation. Yet, China is consolidating power over the South China Sea and the Indian Ocean with an eye on India, something that comes out clearly in a secret memorandum issued by the director of the General Logistic Department of the PLA: 'We can no longer accept the Indian Ocean as only an ocean of the Indians ... We are taking armed conflicts in the region into account.'[38]

China has deployed its Jin-class submarines at a submarine base near Sanya in the southern tip of Hainan Island in South China Sea, raising alarm in India as the base is merely 1,200 nautical miles from the Strait of Malacca. The base will be its closest access point to the Indian Ocean. The base also has an underground facility that can hide the movement of submarines, making them difficult to detect.[39] The concentration of strategic naval forces at Sanya will further propel China towards a consolidation of its control over the surrounding Indian Ocean region. The presence of access tunnels on the mouth of the deep-water base is particularly troubling for India as it will have strategic implications, allowing China to interdict shipping at the three crucial choke points in the Indian Ocean. The choice of Hainan is poor, but no alternatives exist as other places are hemmed in by islands. So China's chief maritime nuclear base is also what is for now her southernmost point. China would want the waters around clear so that, among other things, no one can track its submarines.

As the ability of China's navy to project power in the Indian Ocean region grows, India is likely to feel even more vulnerable, despite enjoying distinct geographical advantages in the area. China's presence there is troubling as it restricts India's freedom to manoeuvre in the region. Of particular note is what has been termed as China's 'string of pearls' strategy that has significantly expanded its strategic depth in India's backyard.[40]

This 'string of pearls' strategy of bases and diplomatic ties includes the Gwadar port in Pakistan, naval outposts in Burma, electronic intelligence gathering facilities on islands in the Bay of Bengal, funding construction of a canal across the Kra Isthmus in Thailand, a military agreement with Cambodia and building up of forces in the South China Sea.[41] Some of these claims are exaggerated, as has been the case with the Chinese naval presence in Burma. The Indian government, for example, had to concede in 2005 that reports of China turning Coco Islands into a naval base were incorrect and that there were indeed no naval bases in Burma.[42] Yet, the

Chinese thrust into the Indian Ocean is gradually becoming more pronounced than before. The Chinese may not have a naval base in Burma but they are involved in the upgradation of infrastructure in the Coco Islands and may be providing some limited technical assistance to Burma. Given that almost 80 per cent of China's oil passes through the Strait of Malacca, it is reluctant to rely on US naval power for unhindered access to energy and so has decided to build up its naval power at choke points along the sea routes from the Persian Gulf to the South China Sea. China is also courting other states in South Asia by building container ports in Bangladesh at Chittagong and in Sri Lanka at Hambantota. Consolidating its access to the Indian Ocean, China has signed an agreement with Sri Lanka to finance the development of the Hambantota Development Zone, which includes a container port, a bunker system, and an oil refinery. It is courting Mauritius and Seychelles to secure a naval foothold in the western Indian Ocean. If China succeeds in getting its way, the Indian Navy, which has been the main security partner of Mauritius, will find itself completely marginalized in the island nation. It is possible that the construction of these ports and facilities around India's periphery by China can be explained away on purely economic and commercial grounds, but in so far as India is concerned this is a policy of containment by other means.

China's diplomatic and military efforts in the Indian Ocean seem to exhibit a desire to project power vis-à-vis competing powers in the region such as the US and

India. China's presence in the Bay of Bengal via roads and ports in Burma and in the Arabian Sea via the Chinese-built port of Gwadar in Pakistan should be a cause of concern for India. With access to crucial port facilities in Egypt, Iran, and Pakistan, China is well poised to secure its interests in the region.

China's involvement in the construction of the deep-sea port of Gwadar has attracted a lot of attention due to its strategic location, about 70 km from the Iranian border and 400 km east of the Strait of Hormuz, a major oil supply route. It has been suggested that it will provide China with a 'listening post' from where it can 'monitor US naval activity in the Persian Gulf, Indian activity in the Arabian Sea, and future US-Indian maritime cooperation in the Indian Ocean'.[43] Though Pakistan's naval capabilities do not, on their own, pose any challenge to India, the combinations of Chinese and Pakistani naval forces can indeed be formidable for India to counter.

It has been suggested that the Chinese government appears 'to have a very clear vision of the future importance of the sea and a sense of the strategic leadership needed to develop maritime interest'.[44] This is reflected in the attempts that China has made in recent years to build up all aspects of its maritime economy and to create one of the world's largest merchant fleets with a port, transport, and shipbuilding infrastructure to match. The Indian Ocean has an important role to play in this effort.

China's aspirations for achieving naval domination of the ocean remain a bit far-fetched in the short to medium term. China would certainly like to play a greater role in the region, and protect and advance its interests, especially commerce, as well as counter India. But given the immense geographical advantages that Indian enjoys in the Indian Ocean, China will have great difficulty in exerting as much sway there as India can. But China's assertion of its naval prowess is raising vexing issues regarding the role of Indian naval power in the Indian Ocean. The Indian and Chinese navies are growing and acquiring the capability to operate at long distances. Maritime friction is likely to grow as the Indian Navy tries to expand its footprint in the South China Sea and the Western Pacific even as the Chinese navy increases its presence in the Indian Ocean.

The Nuclear Dimension

China remains the only major power in the world that refuses to discuss nuclear issues with India for fear that this might imply a de facto recognition of India's status as a nuclear power. It continues to insist on the sanctity of UN resolution 1172 which calls for India (and Pakistan) to give up its nuclear weapons programme and join the Nuclear Non-Proliferation Treaty (NPT) as a non-nuclear weapon state.[45] This was reflected in China's lack of response to former Indian foreign minister Natwar Singh's rather fantastical proposal of a common nuclear doctrine for China, India, and Pakistan. For the same reason that China would not like to get into any sort of nuclear dialogue with India, it also refuses to discuss nuclear confidence building and risk reduction measures with India. It is interesting that a large section of China's political and military elite views India's nuclear tests in 1998 not as an attempt by India to address its security concerns but rather an attempt by the US to contain China in so far as the US 'allowed' India to go nuclear.[46]

The US-India civilian nuclear energy cooperation pact came as a shock to Beijing. China made every possible effort to scuttle the deal till the last minute. It made its displeasure with the nuclear pact clear by asking India to sign the NPT and dismantle its nuclear weapons. The official Xinhua news agency of China commented that the US-India nuclear agreement 'will set a bad example for other countries'.[47] Since the US-India deal is in many ways a recognition of India's rising global profile, China, not surprisingly, was not very happy with the outcome and quickly declared that it would be selling new nuclear reactors to Pakistan. It was a not-so-subtle message to the US that if Washington decided to play favourites, China also retained the same right.

China's action conveyed to India that even as India tries hard to break out of the straitjacket of being a South Asian power by forging a strategic partnership with the US, China will do its utmost to contain India by building up its neighbouring adversaries. For long China was a vociferous critic of the nuclear regime. It signed the NPT only in 1992 and was admitted to the NSG in 2004 despite its abysmal non-proliferation credentials. The reasons for Chinese opposition to the nuclear deal were clearly underlined in an article in the

August 2007 issue of the *Renmin Jiabao*: 'The US-India nuclear agreement has strong symbolic significance (for) India in achieving its dream of becoming a powerful nation ... In fact, the purpose of the US to sign a civilian nuclear agreement with India is to enclose India into its global partners' camp. This fits in with India's wishes.'

Beijing viewed the nuclear deal through the lens of global balance of power and was perturbed about the US desire to build India as a balancer in the region. China was opposed to an exemption to India from the NSG guidelines, even threatening to walk out of the NSG proceedings at Vienna in 2008 in its attempts to derail negotiations at the eleventh hour. The Chinese leadership refused to receive the Indian prime minister's call during the crisis. Only when the other states were persuaded by the US to support the deal and China realized that it would be the last state standing did it back off from its obstructionist stance.

To counter the US-India nuclear pact, China has decided to allow its state entities to supply two new nuclear reactors to Pakistan. Chinese authorities have confirmed that the state-owned China National Nuclear Cooperation has signed an agreement with Pakistan for the two reactors at the Chashma site – Chashma III and Chashma IV – in addition to the two it is already working on in Pakistan. This action of China will be in clear violation of the NSG guidelines that forbid nuclear transfers to countries that are not signatories to the NPT or do not adhere to comprehensive international safeguards on their nuclear programme. China has suggested that 'there are compelling political reasons concerning the stability of South Asia to justify the exports', echoing Pakistan's oft-repeated complaint that the US-India nuclear pact has upset stability in the region by assisting India's strategic programme. Unlike the much debated US-India nuclear pact, the Sino-Pakistani agreement is shrouded in secrecy with Beijing even ready to short-circuit the NSG process.[48] The decision to supply reactors to Pakistan, a non-signatory to the NPT and with a record of dealing with North Korea, Iran and Libya, reflects China's growing diplomatic confidence and underscores its view of Pakistan as a prized South Asian strategic power.

The Pakistani nuclear weapons programme is essentially an extension of the Chinese one. China's crucial role in the development of Pakistan's nuclear infrastructure is well documented. Although China has long denied helping any nation attain a nuclear capability, the father of Pakistan's nuclear weapons programme, Abdul Qadeer Khan, himself has acknowledged the crucial role China has played in his nation's nuclear weaponization by gifting 50 kg of weapon-grade enriched uranium, drawings of nuclear weapons and tons of uranium hexafluoride for Pakistan's centrifuges.[49] This is perhaps the only case where a nuclear weapon state has actually passed on weapons grade fissile material as well as a bomb design to a non-nuclear weapon state. The Sino-Pakistan collusion on nuclear issues has continued despite China being a signatory to the NPT.

Moreover, while both India and China have a no-first-use nuclear doctrine, China's doctrine is not applicable to India as India is not a party to the NPT. China's has changed its 'minimum nuclear doctrine' to 'limited nuclear doctrine', suggesting a nuclear warfighting capability. It has been estimated that the Chinese nuclear arsenal of about 500 warheads comprises 200 strategic warheads while the rest are of tactical nature. And those tactical warheads are deployed at about twenty locations in China, including Tibet, and well integrated at the operational level. On the other hand, India's no-first-use pledge and minimum deterrence posture have precluded the possession of tactical nuclear weapons, leading to a serious operational shortcoming as well as depriving India of an appropriate level of deterrence against China.[50] India may well have to attain parity with China's strategic nuclear forces in order to successfully counter its aggressive coercive bargaining.[51]

China is simultaneously pursuing a qualitative and quantitative transformation of its nuclear infrastructure. With an obvious eye towards countering the proposed US ballistic missile defence, China plans to deploy new road-mobile, solid-fuelled, long-range missiles over the next several years. It has been pointed out that China is now prepared to consider using nuclear weapons in a so-called pre-emptive counterattack, raising doubts about it sticking to a no-first-use nuclear policy.[52] Among the five nuclear powers, it is China that is making the most dramatic advances in its nuclear force with the introduction and deployment of new-generation land-based ballistic missiles and nuclear submarines.[53]

TERRITORIAL ISSUES

Even as China has solved most of its territorial disputes with other countries, it is reluctant to move ahead with India on border issues. The entire 4,057 km Sino-Indian frontier is in dispute, with India and China the only known neighbours not to be separated even by a mutually defined Line of Control. And the fact that China is even discussing border issues with India is often portrayed by the Indian government as a great concession on the part of China. India remains satisfied with the 'positive' and 'satisfactory' Joint Working Group negotiations on the boundary issue. Despite the need for an expeditious demarcation of the Line of Actual Control, the talks seem to be continuing endlessly and the momentum of the talks itself seems to have flagged. Both sides claim that they seek a 'fair, reasonable and mutually acceptable settlement' to the boundary question, but the negotiations lack direction and any sense of purpose.

The McMahon line is an imaginary border, now considered as the Line of Actual Control. It has not been physically demarcated on the ground and on military maps. India accuses China of illegally occupying more than 14,000 sq. miles of its territory on its northern border in Kashmir while China lays claim to more than 34,000 sq. miles of India's north-eastern state of Arunachal Pradesh. After claiming Tawang on the pretext that it is the birthplace of the sixth Dalai Lama, China has changed its posture to demand the whole of Arunachal Pradesh. China has refused to issue visas to people from Arunachal Pradesh and in some cases decided to issue visas by stapling in passports, arguing that the passport holders belong to a 'sensitive' region.[54]

China has been reluctant to exchange maps even of the settled sectors of the boundary until the entire boundary is agreed upon, thereby keeping the settlement of the boundary dispute in abeyance for a more 'opportune' moment. After a lot of cajoling from India, the maps of the non-contentious middle sector got exchanged, but nothing has happened on the western and eastern fronts. Even the middle sector, considered settled, came back in dispute when China staked claim to a 2.1 sq. km territory, Finger Area. China is seeking major concessions in the eastern sector of the boundary, especially on the Tawang tract, while India is not in a position to part with Tawang. A breakthrough on this issue seems to be the key to the larger boundary settlement. China has had no compunction in telling India that it should be prepared to give substantial concessions in the eastern and western sectors on the LAC to resolve the boundary dispute, even as it sought a regional trade agreement and market economy status from India.[55]

Beijing has gone back on its word on not pressing for exchange of territories that have settled populations, a principle that was codified in an agreement on political parameters for the resolution of the boundary dispute signed by Manmohan Singh and Wen Jiabao in 2005. India construed this principle as Chinese willingness to give up its claims on Arunachal Pradesh, but of course

China had no such intention. China has adopted shifting positions on the border issue, time and again enunciating new principles but not explaining them. This deliberate opacity and codification of even new principles keep Indian interlocutors in a perpetual state of uncertainty, even as the façade of negotiations continues.

India has failed to limit China's military use of Tibet despite its great implications for Indian security, even as Tibet has become a platform for the projection of Chinese military power. China's policy of militarizing Tibet is aimed at cornering India. Not only has China pumped in infrastructural investments worth billions of dollars in developing roads, railways, airfields, and hydroelectric and geothermal stations, leading to a huge influx of Han Chinese in Tibet, it is also rapidly expanding the logistical capabilities of its armed forces including its air capability, there. It now has the ability to move as many as twenty-one divisions in the event of an emergency.[56]

India's tacit support to the Dalai Lama's government-in-exile has failed to have much of an impact either on China or on the international community. Today even the Dalai Lama seems to have given up his dream of an independent Tibet and appears ready to talk to the Chinese as he realizes that in a few years' time Tibet might get overwhelmed with the Han population and Tibetans themselves might become a minority.

The Dalai Lama has offered major political concessions to Beijing. He has vowed not to seek the independence of Tibet from China and declared that he sees no political role for himself or the institution of the Dalai

Lama in Tibet after a mutually satisfactory agreement on the future of the region is worked out with Beijing.[57] Encouraged by the growing isolation of Tibetans, the Chinese have not been satisfied even by this gesture and have asked the Dalai Lama to genuinely renounce Tibetan independence and acknowledge Tibet as an inseparable part of China if the dialogue is to move forward.[58] Formal negotiations between the Dalai Lama and the Chinese government began in 2002. After several rounds of talks, nothing seems to have been achieved. In fact, the Chinese authorities have only hardened their position.

While the Dalai Lama has been willing to accept Tibet's autonomous future within China, Beijing wants him to explicitly underline that Tibet has always been a part of China. This is something that the Dalai Lama refuses to do. For Beijing, Dalai Lama is 'a jackal in Buddhist monk's robes, an evil spirit with the human face and the heart of a beast'. So, it is just waiting for the Dalai Lama to die and has already selected its own Panchen Lama, the second-ranking figure in Tibetan Buddhism.

The Tibetans have seen a gradual erosion of their freedoms since the PLA arrived in 1951 and in all likelihood will lose much of their unique cultural identity within a generation. The influx of Han Chinese and a perception that China is destroying their way of life is leading to growing frustration with Beijing despite the economic growth experienced by the region in recent years. Non-Han minorities are just around 9 per cent of China's population and yet China has found it difficult to deal with them in a dignified manner. The intractability of the Tibetan problem, highlighted by the Tibetan uprising in the spring of 2007 and the subsequent Chinese crackdown, is leading more and more Tibetan exiles, especially of the younger generation, to question the Dalai Lama's non-violent approach. There are continuing pressures on the government-in-exile to start a formal independence movement. As of now the Dalai Lama's 'middle way' approach retains its support but that support is waning fast. The world, however, is not willing to confront China on any issue, much less Tibet. Encouraged by the international community's silence, China launched its 'strike hard' campaign to detain those involved in the Tibetan riots in 2008, sending a warning signal to others who support Tibetan independence. This has been followed up by a wider crackdown on prominent Tibetan artists, intellectuals, business people, and students around China, including those who have nothing to do with politics, on charges of subverting state power.[59] Tibet lies at the heart of the deep distrust between India and China. It remains unclear what more India can do to reassure China that it has no designs on Tibet. New Delhi has always insisted that the Dalai Lama is not a mere political dissident but a spiritual leader widely revered in India. By failing to use Tibet as a bargaining chip, India has been perpetually on the defensive, losing ever more territory to the Chinese. As has been rightly pointed out, India is yet to fully comprehend the Chinese modus operandi of promising a peaceful settlement and then employing force to change facts on the ground.[60]

The year 2010 marks sixty years of the Chinese occupation of Tibet. The Chinese conquest of Tibet in 1951 should have led to a fundamental reassessment regarding China's motives with respect to India. Yet, even in 2010, China's gradual encroachment of Indian territory continues to surprise the Indian leadership. India is not being idealistic when it ignores the suppression of the Tibetans. India is not being realistic when it ignores the implications of China's Tibet policy for Indian national security. Asking its ministers to stay away from a function felicitating the Dalai Lama, the Cabinet Secretary wrote to them that attending the function was 'not in conformity with the foreign policy of the government'.[61] No wonder, even the Dalai Lama has termed India's approach as 'overcautious'.

China has vigorously asserted its old claims along the border with India and has combined it with aggressive patrolling. Violating the 1993 India-China agreement on peace and tranquillity on the Line of Actual Control, the Chinese troops have been engaging the Indian troops in verbal abuses, asking them to leave their own territory.[62] Even as India considered the Sikkim border issue settled, repeated Chinese incursions in the Finger Area in northern Sikkim in the past few years are aimed at opening a fresh front against India.[63] Beijing has decided to put the historically undisputed border with Sikkim back in contestation. Concerns are growing about covert Chinese intrusions into Indian territory to strengthen its claims on the disputed border areas.[64] Chinese forces are regularly intruding into Bhutanese territory at the tri-junction with India and destroying

Indian Army posts. These incursions are strategically aimed as they are precariously close to India's 'chicken neck' – the Siliguri corridor which links the north-east passage. Chinese intrusions into the non-delineated parts of Bhutan's northern border with Tibet are also aimed at forcing Bhutan to settle its boundary issue with China. China's blocking of the ADB loan to India in 2009 was the first time China used a multilateral institution to influence a territorial dispute.

It is indeed unfortunate that state governments in Sikkim and Arunachal Pradesh have to push for better air, rail and road connectivity when New Delhi should have been looking at these projects from a strategic perspective. India's poor record on border management has continued since the 1950s. More than sixty years after independence, the Indian defence minister finds himself startled at the differences between Chinese and Indian infrastructure along the border.[65] China's lead in developing key infrastructure like roads, railway lines and air links along the border areas is unmistakable. It is not enough to merely keep repeating that Arunachal Pradesh is part of India, as was underscored by the sarcastic demand from the Member of Parliament from Arunachal that his state should be allowed to get a rail link from China.[66]

China's rapid expansion and modernization of its transport infrastructure across the border is forcing India to respond though India is already decades behind. The build-up of infrastructure in Tibet should have rung alarm bells in Delhi long back but no response was forthcoming. China's transportation modernization plans across the Himalayas had been evident for decades. Yet India chose to be lackadaisical in its approach without demonstrating the sense of urgency that this critical factor in national security demanded. Improved infrastructure helped China to rapidly deploy troops in Tibet when the riots broke out in 2008. The railway link between Beijing and Lhasa further tightens China's grip on Tibet. China's ambition is to extend the Beijing-Lhasa rail line to Yatung just a few miles from Sikkim's Nathu La and subsequently extend this to Nyingchi, north of Arunachal Pradesh, at the tri-junction with Myanmar.[67] China's ambitions about the development of its border areas contrast vividly with India's tentative stance on infrastructure development.

When confronted with the issue of Chinese incursions, the Indian government has tended to react with banalities, first playing down incidents and later acknowledging that something is going on, but never fully levelling with the Indian people as to what really is going on at the borders. Defying credulity, the former external affairs minister, Pranab Mukherjee once suggested, 'It is not unusual (but) it has not suddenly increased.'[68] Yet, it is now being officially recognized that the area along the Line of Actual Control with China has shrunk, with India losing a substantial amount of land over the last two decades.[69] The government also threatened to file FIRs against those reporting on Chinese firings across the border, further undermining its own credibility. The government's attempt to downplay Chinese aggressiveness is no longer working. More damagingly, since there is no transparency on the boundary issue, the field is open to the media and the chattering classes to put their own spin on this issue. When the media became out of control, the Indian prime minister had to intervene to reassure the nation that there was no reason for concern on the China front and the media was hyping the issue.[70] In the information age this inability to effectively use the media for strategic ends continues to undermine the Indian government's position by making it difficult to comprehend its position on crucial issues.

Clearly, the divergence between China and India at the bilateral level has been growing fast and furious. What Indian policy makers who dream of India as a rising global power should worry about even more is the global profile of China. Though the world tends to bracket China and India together, compared to China, India's global profile is close to non-existent.

4

A CONTRAST IN GLOBAL PROFILES

CHINA IS TODAY an emerging superpower with growing economic and political interests in almost every part of the globe that need to be preserved and enhanced. The rapidity of the rise in China's profile around the world has surprised many, though it should have been obvious to those following its economic trajectory. As China became economically powerful, it was bound to become ambitious and assert its profile across the globe. This is a trend that all great powers have followed throughout history.[1] China's foreign policy strategy is aimed at protecting the country from external threats as it pursues its geopolitical interests, thereby allowing it to continue with the reforms of its economy and acquire comprehensive national power without having to deal with the impediments and distractions of security competition.[2]

For long, China had shied away from playing the kind of active role in international affairs that would seem commensurate with its economic weight. This was primarily because the Chinese political leadership had made a strategic choice of concentrating on economic development at home without attempting to play a more interventionist global role lest it distract them from their number one priority of economic development. But the last few years have seen China shunning this reticence and signalling that it is no longer willing to watch events unfold from the sidelines, thereby accepting its new status as a global player of significance. China is expanding its presence and deepening its engagement with states in all parts of the world beyond the Asia-Pacific, including Latin America, Africa and the Middle East.

During the early years of the Cold War, China viewed itself at the vanguard of the revolutionary communist ideology and made an attempt to spread it throughout the world, particularly in the Third World. However, already by the 1960s it became clear that this policy was a non-starter in most parts of the world. Though it tried to project itself as a leader of the Third World and provided support to several left-wing regimes, it was the Soviets to which these states turned if they needed support against the West. Given these challenges, China focused on developing ties with smaller militant groups, rather than state actors, devising a policy that became known as the 'radicalism of impotence',[3] giving China nothing substantive but propaganda advantages in the region. With the end of the Cold War, China emerged as a major global economic player and other states started taking China more seriously. Meanwhile, China also started becoming more ambitious in defining its strategic agenda even as its primary concern remained global and regional stability, which were seen as essential for its economic development. Over time, China's foreign policy towards the Third World, despite its stated revolutionary aims, became evolutionary and pragmatic as trade emerged as China's priority, and other states became more tactful in their dealings with China, benefiting from its material aid and learning from its developmental trajectory.[4]

This newfound foreign engagement is also the result of a realization in China that an active international role is necessary in order to maintain its double-digit rates of growth. A significant proportion of oil and other natural resources needed to run the economy are imported by China and so wooing of nations that are rich in energy and other raw materials becomes paramount. Moreover, China also has to keep searching for new markets for its expanding manufacturing sector.

China is defending its interests in various parts of the world through the time-tested means employed by great powers that include large volumes of economic assistance, subsidizing companies in capturing export markets, supporting governments that do business with it and selling arms to such regimes that might use them against their internal and regional adversaries.

China's mix of authoritarianism and rapid economic growth is attractive to states with fragile political and economic institutions and whose relations with the West tend to be ambivalent. Beijing has begun to emerge as a political and economic alternative to the West in many parts of the world. Politically, China intends to build diplomatic support among nations for its priorities at the UN and other global institutions where its interests are increasingly diverging from the West. While not overtly balancing against the US preponderance by forming external alliances, China is most likely to try to use 'soft balancing' to contain the US might by entangling it in a web of international institutional rules and procedures or ad hoc diplomatic manoeuvres.[5] China's growing engagement with the rest of the world also helps it to further marginalize Taiwan as the number of states extending diplomatic recognition to it dwindles under Chinese resurgence.

Not surprisingly, China is using all the levers at its disposal to raise its profile in far-flung regions of the world. China's trade surplus is mounting inexorably, as is its stash of foreign exchange – the essence of influence in today's world. China is using its foreign currency reserves to cement diplomatic alliances, secure access to natural resources and to garner business for its companies even as it talks of a 'harmonious world' order to counter the perception that a rising China is a threat to the world. China has quietly reoriented its foreign policy to emerge as a new advocate of 'soft power' – a combination of diplomatic outreach, cultural attractiveness and economic might that helps a nation persuade other countries to follow its lead.[6] China's once suspicious neighbours have been drawn into its sphere of economic influence and it has been successful in extending its influence in places as far apart as South-east Asia, Latin

America, and Africa, often in quest for oil and other natural resources to fuel the Chinese industrial revolution.

SHIFTING CENTRE OF GRAVITY IN THE ASIA-PACIFIC

There is a new robustness in China's dealings with the world. It was China that led the way out of the financial crisis, helping the West to recover from the deepest depression since the Second World War. China enjoys huge trade surpluses with the West and holds more than $2 trillion in foreign reserves. The apparent weakening of the West because of the financial crisis is viewed as an opportunity by many in China to strengthen its own position. China is increasingly behaving like a great power. This is in stark contrast to the cautious approach in international affairs that has been its trademark so far. It was based on Deng Xiaoping's four principles: keeping a low profile, not taking the lead, watching developments patiently, and keeping capabilities hidden. But today the swagger in the Chinese approach to the world is apparent in the suggestion emanating from some Chinese quarters that China would not hesitate to sell off US Treasury bills if Washington dares to anger Beijing on Tibet and Taiwan. The financial crisis has presented Beijing with an opportunity to assert itself and the Obama administration's kowtowing to the Chinese early on in its term merely cemented that perception around the world. The US faces the biggest challenge in the Asia-Pacific where the rise of China has upended the traditional balance of power.

It is almost conventional wisdom now that the centre of gravity of global politics is shifting from the Atlantic to the Pacific with the rise of China and India, gradual assertion by Japan of its military profile, and a significant shift in the US global force posture in favour of the Asia-Pacific region.[7] The world seems to be entering into a 'post-American' era and the international system is trying to come to grips with the rise of China and all that it implies for global peace and stability.[8] While realizing fully well that it would take decades to seriously compete with the US for true global hegemony, China has focused its strategic energies on Asia-Pacific. Its foreign policy is aimed at enhancing its economic and military prowess to achieve hegemony there. China's emphasis on projecting its rise as peaceful is aimed at allaying the concerns of its neighbours lest they try to counterbalance its growing influence.[9] Its readiness to negotiate with other regional states and to be an economically 'responsible' power is also a signal to other states that there are greater benefits in going along with rather than opposing its rise in any manner. China realizes that it has thrived because it devotes itself to economic development while letting the US police the region.

While the US still remains the predominant power in Asia-Pacific, China is reshaping the strategic environment in the region. China, India and Japan have long been viewed as the states with a potential for great-power status with inherent capacities to influence international economic, political and military systems, but it is only in the last few years that these projections have come closer to be realized.[10] For more than a century it was Japan that dominated Asia, first as an imperial power and then as the first Asian economy to achieve Western levels of economic development. It is China's turn now, which while declaring that it will be focusing on development for the next decade or so, is actively pursuing policies of preventing the rise of other regional powers such as India and Japan, or at least to limit their development relative to itself. China's resurgence is altering the power balance across Asia-Pacific and in the absence of effective regional institutions, the region is now at least as volatile as during the Cold War.[11]

Despite significant economic and trade ties between China and Japan, underscored by China replacing the US as Japan's biggest trading partner in 2004, political tensions between the two have increased, especially over the differing interpretations of history by the two nations.[12] There was a public outcry in China in 2005 when Japan's education ministry approved history textbooks that were said to whitewash Japan's militarism in Asia during the first half of the last century. It is argued that about 200,000 to 300,000 Chinese were killed during the Japanese occupation of Nanjing that began in 1937. China asked Japan to take responsibility for the unrest in various cities that erupted with some subtle manipulation by China's political establishment.[13]

Japan, meanwhile, asked for an apology of its own from China for violent attacks against Japanese government offices and businesses there. It also did not help when Tokyo's high court rejected an appeal for compensation by Chinese survivors of biological-warfare experiments conducted by Japan during the Second World War.[14] But it would be a mistake to view these Sino-Japanese tensions merely through the prism of history. It is also about the future of Asian balance of power. At its foundation, what is fuelling these tensions is a strategic rivalry as China's power expands across Asia and Japan redefines its regional military role in close cooperation with the US and other regional actors.

The George W. Bush administration had backed the notion of a more assertive Japan, viewing Tokyo as an increasingly important partner at a time of dwindling support for the administration's policies among US allies. The US faces a prospect of an emerging power transition involving China and the most consequential challenge for the US foreign policy in the coming decades will be to deal with this prospect. With this in mind, the US seems to be pursuing a policy of engaging China while simultaneously investing in increasing the power of other states located along China's periphery. This has involved not only reinvigorating its existing alliance with Japan but also reaching out to new partners such as India.[15] Japan and the US signed a pact to enhance cooperation on a ballistic missile defence system in 2004 that is due to be fully operational by 2011. The US has also encouraged Japan to forge close political and strategic ties with states such as India and Australia.

Yet, China's growing clout was on display when in its early days the Obama administration toyed with the idea of G-2, a global condominium of the US and

China whereby China can be expected to look after and 'manage' Asia-Pacific. This was enough to shake up the US allies in the region from their slumber. Realizing that their security concerns were being sidelined in Washington, Tokyo, Seoul and Canberra made a concerted effort to make the new administration realize that such an arrangement would permanently marginalize the US in the strategic landscape of the region. Moreover, major players in the region started re-evaluating their own security doctrines. Even Kevin Rudd, the former Australian prime minister and a great Sinophile, was forced to come up with a security strategy for Australia that sought to hedge its bets with respect to the potential threat from China and an unwillingness on the part of the US to play the role of regional balancer.

The talk then turned to G-3 – a forum that would bring together the US, China and Japan – primarily aimed at pacifying Japan. Given the heavy US economic dependence on Beijing, a G-2 made some sense for the US, but it marginalized American allies in the region. India was perhaps the worst hit. From being viewed as a rising power and a balancer in the Asia-Pacific, India was back to being seen as a South Asian actor whose only relevance for the US was in making sure that Pakistan fought the Taliban with full vigour without getting preoccupied in Kashmir. The smaller countries of East and South-east Asia, not to mention India's immediate neighbours who are being wooed by China, could not but note the shifting balance of power that Washington's manoeuvring signalled and adjusted their own policies. Would the countries be as willing to build stronger ties with India if they see it being marginalized by the US?

The chimera of 'Chimerica', however, soon faced its inevitable demise. After the Obama administration notified the US Congress that it planned to sell weapon systems to Taiwan worth $6.4 billion, China was markedly aggressive in reacting to these developments as compared to the past. Not only was the US ambassador called in by the Chinese government to protest against the arms sales and warned of serious repercussions if the deal went through, China also cancelled some of its military exchange programmes with the US and announced sanctions against the American companies that are supplying weapon systems to Taiwan.

This announcement of sanctions came as a surprise. For the first time, China decided to penalize US companies that were engaged in commercial arms transactions and were not in violation of global non-proliferation norms.[16]

The China of today is not the China of yore. It is ready and willing to push back the US on issues of vital national interests. It views itself as a major global player and therefore is reluctant to be viewed as a pushover any more. Beijing's traditional deference to Washington on major economic and strategic affairs is gone. Instaed, there is a new assertiveness in diplomatic and military affairs. China publicly hectored the White House envoy, Todd Stern, during the conference on climate change at Copenhagen in December 2009 and refused to give an inch to the West during the negotiations. China also forced the organizers of the 2010 World Economic

Forum in Davos not to take up the issues of cyber security and internet freedom despite it being of interest to the Western governments and businesses. And it was at the 2009 World Economic Forum that the Chinese premier had lectured the US on how to manage its economy better. To assert its growing leverage over the US, China has even signalled its interest in a substitute for the dollar in the form of IMF Special Drawing Rights or even gold. And senior PLA officers have openly demanded that their government sell some US bonds to punish Washington for its 'anti-China' policies.

The West, meanwhile, is souring on China. Gone is the talk of China as a responsible stakeholder in the international system. Instead, Google's high-profile public spat with Beijing is being seen as symptomatic of the problems that China's rise continues to generate for global norms set by the West. China's undervalued remnibi is no longer a problem solely for the US, but the Chinese behaviour is questioning the very foundations of the global trade regime. China has failed to play a constructive role in finding a solution to the North Korean and Iranian nuclear issues, much to the consternation of the West, and has in fact made it impossible for the international community to resolve these dangerous flashpoints. There is a fear that China might soon become the pre-eminent world power without even the patina of democracy, with grave consequences for the global order.

The rise of China is shaking up the security dynamic in Asia-Pacific and the regional states are trying to calibrate their ties with China. This has already put the

US-Japan relationship, which has been the cornerstone of the East Asian security architecture since the end of the Second World War, under severe strain. Bilateral disputes between Japan and the US are growing, while China has now surpassed the US as Japan's major trading partner. Meanwhile, the South-east Asian countries are getting ever more closely intertwined with China economically and are finding it difficult to cross swords with it. Even Taiwan wants to conclude a free trade agreement with China at the earliest. Once the China-ASEAN Free Trade Agreement becomes operational, Taiwan's export-dependent economy will be left at a competitive disadvantage.

China is angling for regional leadership in Asia and the contest among various powers is becoming ever more interesting. Beijing is pushing for a trade pact that would include ASEAN's ten members together with China, Japan and South Korea. In an attempt to counterbalance Beijing's growing clout, Japan is proposing a broader 'East Asian Community' that would add Australia, New Zealand and India to the ASEAN+3 arrangement.

Despite the growing economic convergence between China and East Asia, China's growing diplomatic and military assertiveness is causing consternation in the region. Beijing has started claiming that the bulk of the South China Sea constitutes Chinese territorial waters, defining it as a 'core national interest', a phrase previously used in reference to Tibet and Taiwan.[17] This has come as a shock to regional states such as the Philippines, Malaysia, Vietnam and Taiwan, who also have territorial claims in those waters. The South China Sea passage is too important to be controlled by a single country and that too by one that is located far away from these waters.

When China suggests that it would like to extend its territorial waters – which usually run to twelve miles – to include the entire exclusive economic zone, which extends 200 miles, it is challenging the fundamental principle of free navigation. All maritime powers, including India, have a national interest in freedom of navigation, open access to Asia's maritime commons and respect for international law in the South China Sea.

As the US has got consumed by its seemingly never-ending 'war on terror' and domestic economic difficulties, China has started making its presence felt beyond its immediate neighbourhood. Nowhere is China's presence more felt and debated than in Africa, where its involvement is being viewed as part of another 'scramble for Africa' comparable to the nineteenth-century exploitation of the region's resources by major Western powers.

THE DRAGON WOOS AFRICA

It almost seems as if Africa is the new El Dorado given the vigour with which China seems to be pursuing the region. Top Chinese officials have been regularly visiting the continent for the last several years underscoring the solid commitment of the communist leadership to make China the principal external partner of the continent. China organized the China-Africa forum with great fanfare in 2006, which was attended by the political leaders of forty-eight of the fifty-three African countries.

It is not without significance that the superpower-in-waiting is asserting its growing political and economic profile in a continent that has often felt neglected by other major global players. China is the second-largest consumer of oil in the world and one-third of China's total crude imports come from Angola, Sudan, Congo, Gabon, Equatorial Guinea, Chad, and Nigeria.[18] Beijing's huge purchases of oil and other resources have made it Africa's third-largest partner, after the US and France. Angola is now the largest exporter of oil to China, even sidelining Saudi Arabia.

A prerequisite for doing serious business with China is to recognize China and sever ties with Taiwan. In its first-ever White Paper on Africa brought out in 2006, China asserted that if African states choose to accept the 'one China principle as the potential foundation for the establishment and development of China's relationship with African countries', China will 'coordinate positions on major international and regional issues and stand for mutual support on major issues concerning state sovereignty, territorial integrity, national dignity, and human rights'.[19] While more than twenty African countries recognized Taiwan in the early 1990s, only four do so now. China's success in luring states away from Taiwan has been remarkable, adding further to that country's isolation in the international system in general and in Africa in particular.[20]

The structural constraints imposed by the Cold War disappeared in the early 1990s, and since then China has gradually tried to increase its clout in Africa more substantively. In the evolving global strategic environment, cultivating economic and diplomatic ties with the African nations has emerged as a major foreign policy priority for China. China's trade with Africa has grown by an astounding 1,000 per cent during the past decade, faster than with any other region except the Middle East, and is expected to touch $100 billion in 2010, surpassing the US trade with the continent.[21]

Countries like Angola, Namibia, Zambia and Ethiopia are now heavily dependent on Chinese largesse. China has targeted Africa's oil-producing states to diversify its sources of oil, signing energy deals with Algeria, Nigeria, Angola, Gabon and Sudan. Angola is China's second-largest trading partner in Africa. This remarkable progress in Angola since the end of its civil war has been attributed to China's growing role in the country.[22] Chinese consumer goods have flooded the markets in Africa and its investment in infrastructure projects has made the Chinese presence ubiquitous. China is investing billions and extending easy loans in exchange for access to resources.

Direct Chinese investment in Africa has already crossed the $6 billion mark, mostly in energy and infrastructure projects. Chinese companies have invested in projects ranging from railways in Angola to telecommunications in Nigeria, even hotels in Sierra Leone, in the last decade. This has resulted in a sustained wooing of Africa by China led by its top decision makers who toured Africa, lobbying for lucrative contracts and promising investments.

The largest China-Africa gathering since the founding of communist China in 1949 was held in 2006, where Chinese and African leaders signed deals worth $1.9 billion, covering telecommunications, infrastructure, insurance, and mineral resources, amid assurances from China that it would not monopolize Africa's resources. China also agreed to extend $1.5 billion in loans and credits to Africa, forgive past debts, and double foreign aid to the continent by 2009. China and the participating nations from Africa also declared a strategic partnership and 'action plan' that charts cooperation in the economy, international affairs, and social development.[23]

For many African nations, the most attractive aspect of Chinese involvement in their continent is its no-strings-attached aid policy. The aid from the West is often linked to good governance and human rights clauses which the political leaders in Africa find unpalatable and describe as 'neo-colonialism', an approach aimed at imposing Western political values on them. China has so far tended to ignore the global lending standards intended to fight corruption in the region. Even the IMF and World Bank see their years of painstaking efforts to arrange conditional debt relief getting undermined by China's unrestricted lending. But China has made 'non-interference in other states' internal affairs' a central tenet of its foreign policy. This has as much to do with making China an attractive partner for the Africans as it has to do with China's own sensitivities towards interference in its domestic politics. Even as the IMF was negotiating structural reforms with the Angolan government in 2004, China stepped in and offered Angola aid without any preconditions, thereby luring Angola away from much-needed reforms.

China's military presence is also growing on the African continent, with Beijing supplying arms to both sides in one of Africa's longest-running conflicts, between Ethiopia and Eritrea. China has also supplied arms to Sudan, Congo, Angola, Sierra Leone and Liberia. China is sending more peacekeeping troops to Africa than ever before, and expanding its military exchanges with various African governments. It is the leading military supplier to Zimbabwe, even as Robert Mugabe has used this military hardware and training mainly to contain growing domestic opposition against his government. Mugabe's 'Look East' policy, initiated a few years back in response to his regime's ostracization by the Western governments for his human rights abuses, has had its biggest success in attracting China to Zimbabwe, so much so that China is now Zimbabwe's second-largest trading partner. More significant, especially in the light of developments in Darfur, China has a military relationship with the Sudanese government and despite the UN arms embargo, this engagement has remained undiminished.

China's soft power is also on the ascendant in Africa. It is being viewed as a land of opportunities and prosperity, replacing the role that the US and Europe have long played in the consciousness of the people of Africa. African students are going to China in larger numbers than ever before. China is leveraging its soft power – culture, investment, academia, foreign aid, public diplomacy – more effectively than before to influence Africa and other regions in the developing world.[24]

While Chinese officials have defended their outreach to Africa by arguing that their aid to countries there actually supports a fundamental human right in Africa, that of the right to development, the question remains if the Chinese strategy is further retarding the development of an already impoverished continent. The Chinese policy of extracting natural resources and raw materials from Africa and selling finished manufactured products back is essentially mercantilist in nature. There is no doubt that a boom in China-Africa trade along with cancellation of debt and aid to African states has proved to be mutually advantageous for China and African elites, but the long-term political and economic consequences of China's increased involvement in Africa might be deleterious.[25] While there is an expectation that Africa and its inhabitants would benefit from the growing involvement of outside powers as they extract resources and provide windfall gains for development, there are concerns that such an approach fuels environmental degradation, economic mismanagement, poverty, and state corruption.

Though opposition to China's policies towards Africa from non-African governments and organizations has been part of the global discourse for some time now, more recently it is from within Africa that voices are rising against many of the Chinese policies. One reason for concern is that China's economic power is strangling African manufacturing while locking up vital resources for years, as the flood of Chinese finished goods to Africa has created a large trade imbalance. Textile mills in various African states, including Nigeria and South

Africa, have closed down under the onslaught of inexpensive Chinese imports, leading to public protests. In a somewhat surprising outburst, former South African president Thabo Mbeki had warned that Africa risked becoming an economic colony of China if the trade imbalance between the continent and the Asian dragon was not rectified soon.[26] There is growing political opposition in Zambia to Chinese purchases of mining concessions, with some accusing it of plundering their nation's natural resources. The perception that China's economic influence is having a negative effect on the domestic labour market and local manufacturing is spreading in several African nations despite the willingness of the political leadership in these states to continue accepting Chinese economic largesse. There have been a string of attacks on Chinese nationals in Africa in recent times, underlining the tenuous nature of its presence in the continent. Yet, it is unlikely that the Chinese presence in Africa is going to dwindle any time soon.

CHINA IN THE MIDDLE EAST

China is fast emerging as a significant actor in the Middle Eastern political landscape. There are a range of factors that have been shaping its policy towards the Middle East in recent years, though China would be reluctant to see the status quo in the region disturbed in the short term as it serves its primary interest of sustaining its high rates of economic growth. Yet, the relative decline of the US in the region might just force

China into making some difficult diplomatic choices very soon.

Much like Africa, China's interest in the Middle East is primarily driven by its economic and energy needs. However, it has not been shy to take advantage of the relative decline in the US influence in the region and calibrate its policy accordingly. This has encouraged China to court rogue regimes and challenge US hegemony, but only so long as this does not impinge on its broader interests with the US. It is not interested in taking on the role that the US plays in the region of maintaining a rough balance of power in the short term. China is challenging the US hegemony, but only very subtly. To the extent the US has lost influence in the region in the last few years, China has been a natural beneficiary of that decline. It doesn't, however, as of now have the capabilities or the willingness to take on the role of the US.

China has become an extremely attractive alternative to states worldwide and in the Middle East in particular that are troubled by American foreign policy's preoccupation with the domestic character of political regimes. As the 2006 US National Security Strategy document makes clear, for the US, 'the fundamental character of regimes matters as much as the distribution of power among the states'. And the goal of American statecraft is 'to help create a world of democratic, well-governed states than can meet the needs of citizens and conduct themselves responsibly in the international system'.[27] This is as much a concern for China as it is for states that have been traditional allies of the US such as Saudi Arabia.

Since the 1980s, the Saudis have sought to tap the Chinese arms market. In 1985, the Saudi government risked Washington's ire to import Chinese CSS-2 nuclear-capable, intermediate-range ballistic missiles with a 3,000 km range. With the CSS-2 becoming obsolete, Riyadh is considering purchase of the upgraded, solid-fuelled CSS-5 and CSS-6 with a range of 1,800 and 600 km respectively.[28] Many Saudi officials, annoyed with US pressure to cease funding Islamist and extremist groups, find Beijing's no-questions-asked policies attractive. Beijing and Riyadh are in one key way alike, in that both seek to take advantage of economic globalization without endangering their political status quo.

Since the late 1990s, China had been urging the international community to lift sanctions against Saddam Hussein's regime in Iraq primarily because it viewed Baghdad as an attractive destination for selling arms and a lucrative source of energy. Though China was critical of the US decision to invade Iraq, it adopted a low-key approach and allowed states like France and Russia to take the lead in opposing US actions in the UN Security Council. Despite its opposition to the occupation in 2003, it was one of the first countries to re-establish relations with the US-backed government that took over after Saddam's fall. As the US got bogged down in Iraq, China became more assertive in pursuing its own agenda. Chinese companies now enjoy stakes in three of the eleven contracts signed by the Iraqi oil ministry, and Beijing successfully renegotiated a $3 billion deal that was signed with Saddam Hussein's regime in 1997 to develop Iraqi oilfields of al-Ahdab.[29]

In a sign that China would like to be taken seriously as an actor in Middle Eastern politics, it appointed its first peace envoy for the region in 2002. Though China would not like a very active role in the peace process, for fear of offending either side, it has made it clear that it too has a stake in the future of the region. At the level of rhetoric, China has long supported the Palestinian cause, but in practical terms, this has not resulted in any material help to the Palestinians. In fact, China's ties with Israel have evolved more rapidly due to the lure that Israeli technical know-how holds for the Chinese. In China, Israel has found a huge market for its defence equipment, while China is able to acquire Western technology to undergird its ambitious military modernization programme. Israel has emerged as China's largest defence supplier after Russia. China remains heavily dependent on Israeli arms and views them as a means to acquire the US-made weapons platforms, something it cannot get from elsewhere.

Yet, China has been eager to build its ties with Hamas, which the West considers a terrorist organization. It invited the then Palestinian foreign minister, Mahmud al-Zahar, a member of Hamas, to the China-Arab Forum in 2006, much to the consternation of Israel and the West. Given its interests on both sides of the divide, China will continue to rely on the West to take a leading role in the Middle East peace process.

China has built close ties with states like Syria and Iran in the region, states that have been deemed 'rogue' by the US. As early as 1994, former President Jiang Zemin had argued that China should oppose 'hegemony' by helping dissident countries like Iran.[30] And that's exactly what China seems to have done. China has been in a defence relationship with Teheran since the 1980s and the list in this relationship has expanded from Cruise missiles to long-range ballistic missiles to assisting Iran's chemical and nuclear weapons programme. Iran hopes to defeat its global isolation by courting China, and China can make use of Iran's energy resources without any real competition. Chinese firms are key suppliers of ballistic- and Cruise-missile-related technologies to Iran as Iran is China's main customer for arms sales, both conventional and WMD (weapons of mass destruction), in the region.[31] China is also helping Iran in pursuing the development of a nuclear fuel cycle for civil and nuclear weapon purposes, despite Beijing's 1997 bilateral commitment to the US to forgo any new nuclear cooperation with Iran. China has also made sure that the West is unable to take any effective coercive measures against Iran on the issue of its nuclear programme even as Iran has continued to ignore the Security Council resolutions.

China's active role in the UN Security Council is also the last defence for several Third World states concerned with American 'hyperpower'. China has increasingly used the institutional framework of the Security Council and the veto power that it enjoys to snub the American agenda. The latest case is Iran where China, along with Russia, has prevented the West from pursuing meaningful actions against the regime there. China also prevented censure of Syria when it refused to cooperate with the UN investigations into the assassination of former

Lebanese prime minister Rafik Hariri. China's ability to stand up to the US is being perceived as a balancer to the American pre-eminence in the region. Most governments in the Middle East are happy to find an alternative to their traditional dependence on Washington and the Chinese are happy to provide a political and diplomatic alternative for states such as Saudi Arabia, which are upset with US pressure to curtail support for Islamist extremism and perceived US interference in domestic affairs.

Additionally, from being a net exporter of oil until 1995, China has emerged as the world's second-largest oil market after the US. More than 51 per cent of China's oil imports originate in the Gulf and soon almost 95 per cent will. China's appetite for oil is only going to grow, and so will its dependence on Middle Eastern sources of energy. Saudi Arabia and Iran between themselves account for around 30 per cent of China's oil imports and so they have emerged as the pivot of China's Middle East policy. Many in China worry about their country being potentially vulnerable to a US blockade of oil shipment from the Persian Gulf. China's exports to the Middle Eastern states have also been increasing in the last few years and it is buying equity stakes in development projects there.

One of the ways in which China has tried to quell unrest in its Muslim-dominated regions is by building ties with the Middle Eastern states, which are the ideological centre of global Islam. States such as Iran and Saudi Arabia have been most active in propagating their version of Islam across the globe by providing resources to various organizations. China feels that it is necessary to have their support if it wants to tackle successfully the Uighur insurgency, even though it is primarily the Central and South Asian states from where Uighur militants have found support. China confronts a seven-million-strong restive Muslim populace in the resource-rich western province of Xinjiang.

The Uighurs, who have been trying to preserve their distinct cultural identity against the Chinese onslaught, have long shown their dissatisfaction with the rule of the Chinese government and have occasionally resorted to violence. China declared itself as an ally of the US in its 'war against terrorism' after 11 September 2001, and since then oppression in Xinjiang has been at an all-time high. Some links of the Uighur militants with transnational Islamist networks, however, have also come to light and China has claimed that training camps in Afghanistan and Pakistan have led to Uighur militants crossing over into Xinjiang from Central Asia. The silence of the Middle Eastern states on the issue of the Chinese government's attitude towards its Muslim population perhaps indicates a measure of success that China has achieved in keeping this issue under control. There was hardly any reaction at the official level in the Islamic world when the ethnic sectarian unrest broke out in Xinjiang Autonomous Region in 2008 and China clamped down strongly.

Overall, China has been very successful in achieving its short- to medium-term goals in the region. It has developed partnerships with major powers such as Saudi Arabia, Iran and Israel that will serve its energy and defence needs in the foreseeable future. And it has been able to do this without having to make any difficult diplomatic choices as the regional stability has been taken care of by the US. With the US facing challenges in the region, the Chinese profile has risen, though the Chinese policy makers are reluctant to assume a broader role as it will complicate the diplomatic balance they maintain in the region.

COURTING AMERICA'S FRIENDS AND ENEMIES

China's forays in America's backyard have been rather impressive and audacious. The US has for long demanded that Latin America should be seen as its sphere of influence, but China is gradually making inroads there. It is vigorously cultivating Latin America with trade, investment, and political interactions. It has announced plans to invest around $100 billion in the continent over the next decade. China is now the region's third-largest trading partner. It is acquiring mineral assets in the continent and expanding security cooperation with regional states. It is filling the void left by the US in recent years in Latin America by opening Confucian centres, enhancing its diplomatic presence and high-level exchanges.[32] Trade between Latin America and China jumped up from $10 billion in 2000 to $140 billion in 2008, driven largely by China's demand for the region's raw materials. China is also a major lender to Latin America. Brazil-China ties are expanding and attracting attention in the US. The partnership involves civilian nuclear energy cooperation, aircraft co-production, and a joint-satellite development programme. China is now Brazil's largest trading partner and has pledged $10 billion in investments in Brazil. Given its water scarcity and vanishing croplands, China is turning to Brazil for the supply of soybeans.[33]

China has also been successful in courting Russia in recent years. A new era in Sino-Russian relations was ushered in with the breaking up of the Soviet Union and the end of the Cold War period. Moreover, as the relations of China and Russia with the US have deteriorated, they have come closer in identifying with each other's foreign policy interests. Russia's ties with China in the areas of defence and military technology remain central to the overall Sino-Russian relationship. This involves short-term Chinese purchase of Russian weapons to long-term cooperation on joint research and development and production of military equipment, including relatively new technologies for ICBM and SLBM production.[34]

China is the Russian defence industry's largest client, with sales estimated to be between $1 and $2 billion of a total of $4 billion.[35] Impressed with the high growth rates of China, Russia has over the last couple of years focused on strengthening the bilateral economic relationship. The emphasis, therefore, has been on increasing bilateral trade in goods and services and cooperation in the energy sector.[36] Trade between the two countries has grown significantly during the past decade, with volume soaring from $6.83 billion in 1996 to $33.4 billion in 2006, as the Chinese demand for Russian industrial and engineering products, civilian nuclear expertise, and oil has galloped.

The importance of the Shanghai Cooperation Organization (SCO) that has evolved into a forum for discussion on regional security and economic issues cannot be overstated for Sino-Russian relations.[37] It has become even more important post–11 September 2001, because growing ethnic nationalism and Islamic fundamentalism are major causes of concern for both countries. Russia and China have been successful in using the strong aversion of the US to terrorism after 11 September for their own ends to tackle Islamic insurgency within their territories. In the post–9/11 environment, the SCO also serves as a means to keep control of Central Asia and limit US influence in the region. In fact, the SCO denounced the misuse of the anti-terror war to target any country and threw its weight behind the UN in an attempt to show its disagreement with the US-led war in Iraq.[38] While there are problems in the Sino-Russian relationship, Russia's decline as an economic power, and China's rise, has altered the balance of power between them. So much so that it is now Russia which is inviting Chinese investments in its far east because of its inability to pursue developmental projects in the region and the need for capital that China can provide.[39]

IN INDIA'S BACKYARD

China's strategy towards South Asia is premised on encircling India and confining it within the geographical coordinates of the region. China has started strengthening its connections with India's neighbouring states by developing infrastructural linkages and is deepening its military and economic engagements with them, allowing it to envision a larger role for itself in the Indian Ocean region. The Chinese strategy of containing India within the confines of South Asia through the use of its proxies started off with Pakistan and has gradually evolved to include other states in the region, including Bangladesh, Sri Lanka and Nepal.

Not surprisingly, China's quiet assertion in India's backyard has allowed various smaller countries to play China off against India. In South Asia, most states are now using the China card to balance against the predominance of India. This is a standard strategy adopted by small states in regional systems that are dominated by two or more major powers.[40] Small states seek to preserve their sovereignty by resorting to strategies that seek to balance major powers locked in an incessant security competition. Such states promote their national interests by not explicitly aligning with any one major power but pursue policies that preserve their independent existence. Such is the case in South Asia too. Forced to exist between their two giant neighbours, the smaller states in South Asia have responded with a careful balancing act.

China has done its best to maintain a rough balance of power in South Asia by preventing India from gaining an upper hand over Pakistan. China has consistently assisted Pakistan's nuclear weapons and ballistic missile programmes to counterbalance India's development of new weapons systems to a point where, according to the US National Intelligence Council estimates, Pakistan has developed an edge over India in strategic delivery systems.

India's preoccupation with Pakistan reduces India to the level of a regional power, while China can claim the status of an Asian and world power. From supplying it nuclear and missile technologies to building its military infrastructure, China has done all it can to build Pakistan as a counterweight to India. And this policy has largely succeeded. While India no longer enjoys its earlier conventional superiority as compared to Pakistan, possession of nuclear weapons by both nations ensures that any step that India takes to strengthen its nuclear weapons profile is viewed by the international community as highly destabilizing in the context of the 'nuclear flashpoint' that South Asia has become for the world. China has thereby been successful in emerging as a 'responsible' global player, despite its questionable nuclear and missile proliferation record, while the international community rails at India for making the world much more dangerous.

China has signed a charter to step up bilateral defence cooperation with Pakistan 'to help maintain peace and stability in South Asia' even as it professes to improve its relations with India. Pakistan has launched the joint production of JF-17 fighter aircraft with China and has concluded an agreement for the construction of four F-22P frigates for the Pakistani navy.[41] Despite Indian objections, China is not only planning to have a rail link with Pakistan through the strategic Karakoram ranges, it is also constructing highways in the disputed Gilgit-Baltistan region in Pakistan-occupied Kashmir. Moreover, even though India and China share similar concerns regarding Islamic terrorism in Kashmir and Xinjiang respectively, China has been rather unwilling to make common cause with India against Pakistan.

China's use of India's neighbours to curtail Indian influence has not been restricted to Pakistan. Be it in Bangladesh, Nepal or Sri Lanka, China has actively sought to contain India all around its periphery. China has announced its intention to develop 'comprehensive and cooperative partnership' with Bangladesh, even offering assistance in the peaceful uses of nuclear energy.[42] By courting Bangladesh, China will be able to get a strategic toehold in India's eastern flank. The development of Chittagong port along the lines of Gwadar in Pakistan is aimed at facilitating China's entry into the Bay of Bengal. Though Chittagong port is apparently being developed for commercial purposes, it could easily be used for staging Chinese naval assets.

Over the years, China's policy towards Nepal has been guided by its larger strategic game plan in South Asia. In the initial years of the Cold War, when Beijing was worried about a possible coming together of India and the US, it treated Nepal cautiously so as not to hurt Indian interests. However, once China gained confidence and international recognition, it went all out to expand its influence in Nepal. By supporting Kathmandu's position in most disputes between India and Nepal, Beijing was able to project itself as a benevolent power. It was also able to upgrade its military ties with Nepal, despite India's stiff resistance. As ethnic tensions have risen in Tibet, China has sought to curb the activities of Tibetan refugees in Nepal.

China's interest and presence in Nepal, however, has gradually expanded and now goes far beyond the Tibet issue. China is projecting its 'soft power' in Nepal by setting up China Study Centres (CSCs) that are being used to promote Chinese values among the Nepalese, who are otherwise tied culturally to India. These centres are emerging as effective instruments in promoting Chinese perspectives on key issues concerning Nepal.[43] China is constructing a 770 km railway line to connect the Tibetan capital of Lhasa with the Nepalese town of Khasa, a move that would connect Nepal to China's national rail network. China has increased its aid to Nepal substantially in the last few years and the trade volume between the two is growing, though the trade balance continues to remain heavily in favour of China. China is trying to address this by providing duty-free access to Nepalese goods. This strategy of providing aid without any conditions and support for building infrastructure is enhancing China's role even as its products are flooding the Nepalese market, replacing Indian ones. By projecting India as a factor of instability and an undue beneficiary of Nepal's resources, China has used Nepalese sensitivities regarding Indian influence to good effect, thereby further undercutting Indian influence in Kathmandu.

India's political and economic influence in Sri Lanka is gradually shrinking even as courting China gives Colombo greater room for diplomatic manoeuvring with New Delhi. It was India's hands-off policy towards Sri Lanka because of the strong domestic Tamil sentiment against supporting Sri Lankan counterinsurgency that allowed China to move in. As the Tamil Tigers came close to defeating the Sri Lankan forces, the island nation asked India for assistance and all India could do was offer financial aid, even as Colombo turned first to Islamabad and then to Beijing for military supplies. By doing this India gave the Mahinda Rajapaksa regime a free hand in defeating the LTTE and with this India's strategic space in Sri Lanka shrank to an all-time low despite its geostrategic advantage and economic clout.[44] Beijing's diplomatic support helped Colombo to deflect Western criticism of its human rights record in defeating the LTTE. China is today Sri Lanka's biggest aid donor and biggest investor, and with a huge influx of Chinese grants and loans, its presence in Sri Lanka is at an all-time high.

Beijing is laying the foundations for its economic integration with its border regions in India, Bhutan and Nepal. China already has a highway to the Nepal border that is capable of transporting tanks. This road-building will allow China to consolidate its economic domination of the region. Plans are on the anvil for cross-border energy pipelines and fibre-optic links with Nepal. China recognizes that by strengthening border infrastructure, it can also expand its political and cultural influence in the subcontinent. And the same infrastructure could well be used to challenge India militarily should the need arise.

For long, the dominant narrative of the South Asian Association for Regional Cooperation (SAARC) has been how the India-Pakistan rivalry hampers its evolution into anything of significance. That is now losing its salience with China's growing dominance of the South

Asian landscape. China entered SAARC as an observer in 2005, supported by most member states. India could do little about it and so acquiesced. Now, much to India's consternation, Pakistan, Bangladesh and Nepal are supporting China's full membership in SAARC.

China's rising profile in South Asia is no news. What is astonishing is the diminishing role of India and the rapidity with which New Delhi is ceding strategic space to Beijing in the subcontinent. Even as China is becoming the largest trade partner of most states in South Asia, including India, New Delhi is busy repeating the old mantra of South Asia being India's exclusive sphere of influence. Of course, no one even takes note of it any more.

Pakistan's all-weather friendship with China is well known, but China's reach in other South Asian states has been extraordinary. Bangladesh and Sri Lanka view India as more interested in creating barriers against their exports than in spurring regional economic integration. India's protectionist tendencies have allowed China to don the mantle of regional economic leader. Instead of India emerging as facilitator of socio-economic development in Sri Lanka, Nepal and Bhutan, it is China's developmental assistance that is having a larger impact.

China, meanwhile, is entering markets in South Asia more aggressively through both trade and investment, improving linkages with the region's countries through treaties and bilateral cooperation. Following this up by building a ring of road and port connections in India's neighbourhood and deepening military engagements with states on India's periphery, China has firmly entrenched itself in India's backyard. Even in Afghanistan, it is the state-owned China Metallurgical Group that has brought the rights to exploit the copper deposits at Aynak, in Logar province, for $3.5 billion.

The breadth and depth of China's growing global profile is staggering. In a few years, China has made its presence felt in almost every part of the world with great fanfare and ruffling not a few feathers in the process. India, meanwhile, is left to play catch-up and to mimic China's policies. So when China organizes its China-Africa Summit, India follows up with its own. When China decides to give a push to a Free Trade Agreement (FTA) with the Gulf Cooperation Council (GCC), India also wakes up to this imperative. It matters little that where the China-Africa summit was attended by forty-eight of the fifty-three African heads of state, the India-Africa summit could only attract fourteen, and where China has twenty-two embassies in western and central Africa, India has only six small missions in the region.[45]

While the Indian government does not see its collision with China in every part of the world as competition, the rest of the world does.[46] And nowhere is this competitive dynamic between China and India more visible than in the realm of energy.

CHINA AND INDIA COLLIDE, ALMOST EVERYWHERE

China is aggressively working to satisfy its energy requirements in the future. Indian attempts notwithstanding, China has clearly left India far behind in so far as its international diplomacy in the energy realm is concerned. Despite all the talk of Sino-Indian cooperation on energy security, the two sides are actually competing aggressively as their energy demands surge. While there have indeed been some attempts at cooperation, engendering a lot of enthusiasm in some quarters, these developments form a small part of a much broader China-India energy relationship, which remains largely competitive, if not conflictual.

China's interest in oil exploration in the Indian Ocean is a matter of strategic concern for India, especially in the context of China's 'string of pearls' strategy of bases and diplomatic ties stretching from the Middle East to southern China.[47] While Bangladesh has granted China exploration rights for developing natural gas fields of its own, friction in India-Bangladesh ties has precluded cooperation between them on the issue of energy. China's activities near the Kenyan port of Mombasa will make India more wary of the impact of its long-term plans.[48]

After India realized that one of its closest neighbours and a major source of natural gas, Myanmar, was drifting towards China, it reversed its decades-old policy of isolating the military junta and has now begun to deal with it directly.[49] New Delhi not only assured investment in developing the Sittwe Port and extended a $20 million credit for renovation of the Thanlyin refinery, it also supported Myanmar against the US censure motion in an attempt to lure the junta to grant preferential treatment to India in the supply of natural gas. But the

Chinese firms were the ones that got preferential treatment in the award of blocks and gas, apparently in recognition of China's steady opposition to the US moves against Myanmar's junta in the UN.[50]

This failure has galvanized India into wooing Yangon even more aggressively. Apart from India's existing infrastructure projects in Myanmar, which include the 160 km India-Myanmar friendship road built by the Border Roads Organization in 2001, India is looking into the possibility of embarking on a second road project and investing in a deep-sea project (Sagar Samridhi) to explore oil and gas in the Bay of Bengal, as well as the Shwe gas pipeline project in western Myanmar. Even as the junta was readying for a violent crackdown on monks and democracy activists in 2007, the Indian petroleum minister was in Yangon signing a production deal for three deep-water exploration blocks off the Rakhine coast. While India did support the UN Human Rights Council resolution against Myanmar, it tried to tone it down to little effect as it tried to balance its democratic credentials with its desire to retain its influence with the military government. Yet, India has found it difficult to counter Chinese influence there, with China selling everything from weapons to food grains to Myanmar.

China and Myanmar are constructing a pipeline to transport Middle Eastern and African crude oil from Myanmar's Arakan coast to China's Yunnan province. This will give China an alternative to the expensive and sometimes dangerous Strait of Malacca by directly supplying energy to its landlocked west. China's proximity to Myanmar's military rulers has enabled it to swing decisions with regard to Myanmar's energy sector in its favour. It is China that has helped the military junta to keep its behaviour off the agenda of the UN Security Council. China is the largest foreign investor in Myanmar's energy sector, with Chinese companies holding stakes in sixteen oil and gas blocks. China's assistance to Myanmar in constructing and improving port facilities on two islands in the Bay of Bengal and the Andaman Sea might be the first step towards securing military base privileges in the Indian Ocean. This can be used as a listening post to gather intelligence on Indian naval operations and as a forward base for future Chinese naval operations in the ocean. China's naval presence in the Indian Ocean is of great strategic consequence for India, even as India's traditional geographic advantages in the ocean are at risk with deepening Chinese involvement in Myanmar.

As the geopolitical importance of Central Asia has increased in recent years, all the major powers have been keen to expand their influence in the region, and India is no exception. It shares many of the interests of other major powers such as the US, Russia, and China, including access to energy resources there, controlling the spread of radical Islam, ensuring political stability, and strengthening of regional economies. But unlike China and Russia, its interests converge with that of the US in Central Asia and some have even suggested that it is in the American interest to have a greater Indian presence there to counter Chinese or Russian involvement.[51]

Central Asia is crucial for India not only because of its oil and gas reserves that India wishes to tap for its energy security but also because other major powers such as the US, Russia, and China have already started competing for influence in the region. India's concern about Chinese influence in Central Asia is reflected in India's desire to become a member of the Shanghai Cooperation Organization (SCO). When India was granted an observer status in the SCO, however, China made sure that Pakistan was also invited, thereby diminishing India's influence.

China has a major geopolitical advantage in Central Asian oil politics. Oil resources in the region are of vital importance to its energy security and will become an important basis for China's future military strategy. In the event of an unexpected military crisis, China would have to rely heavily on oil resources in the region to sustain military operations. The extension of the pan-Asian global energy bridge from Central Asia to Iran would link China to the Middle East.[52] This lifeline from the Caspian Sea to China, incorporating the Middle East, would most benefit China's long-term strategic energy security policy. It would leave China in a much less vulnerable position with respect to both oil reserve depletion and transportation risks. By drastically shifting the most important and busiest global energy artery from the Strait of Malacca to a line across mainland China, the creation of new geopolitical tendencies inside Asia would be inevitable. China would undoubtedly benefit from such a pivotal geostrategic position, particularly as its coastal regions would serve as the refining link between Middle Eastern and Central Asian crude oil – and the Asian-Pacific market.[53]

Chinese aspirations as an 'energy bridge' in Central Asia are long term and will require massive international investment in pipeline infrastructure and coastal refineries. The China National Petroleum Corporation (CNPC) has an oil-swap agreement with Iran. Oil purchased by China from the Uzen oilfield in Kazakhstan is pumped to a refinery near Teheran, with China receiving an equivalent amount of Iranian crude exported from Iran's Gulf coast. China's other deal with Kazakhstan includes a commitment to build a 3,000 km pipeline from the oilfields to the Xinjiang province of China, and a 250 km pipeline to the border of Iran (via Turkmenistan).[54]

Indian and Chinese state-owned oil companies were engaged in a bidding war to acquire a Canadian company with oilfields in Kazakhstan. The CNPC won the bid against India's ONGC after offering a higher sum for Petro Kazakhstan. The Caspian Sea region in Central Asia is another region that is going to see major powers, including China and India, jostling for influence, given its new-found importance as a still-growing source of oil and gas. The area is distant from world markets, generating uncertainty whether Caspian oil will increasingly be sent east or will continue to flow west through Russia or Turkey. In all probability, China is likely to emerge as a new energy hub for Caspian oil and more pipelines will be built to western China.

The ONGC has a 20 per cent stake in exploration and development of the Sakhalin-I oil and gas fields in Russia and has been keen to import natural gas from

Sakhalin. But China outmanoeuvred India by offering a $6 billion loan to the Russian oil company, Rosneft, which then asked India to outbid China if it wanted to be considered for the exports.[55] India's ONGC Videsh Ltd (OVL) also lost out to China in the acquisition of BP's oil assets in Russia. In one of the first big-ticket oil asset acquisitions by China in Russia, TNK-BP, which controls the OAO Udmurtneft fields, decided to opt for China's Sinopec in place of OVL. Though India has expressed its desire to buy nearly a quarter of its annual oil imports in the next decade from Russia, and Russia plans to increase the share of its energy exports to Asia from the current 5 per cent to around 25 per cent, India will have to compete with other Asian nations, most significantly China, which are as eager to court Russia.[56] While the Chinese have a natural advantage of having a common border with Russia, their diplomacy also seems to be more proactive.

Russia could become an important supplier of oil to China in the coming years. The two states have performed a feasibility study on a $1.6 billion, 2,200 km oil pipeline project to bring Serbian oil to north-east China, which the Chinese government views as one way of alleviating its dependence on oil supplies from the Middle East.[57] Russia is a world-class gas producer, which fits well into the Chinese strategy of diversifying its energy requirements. For such a venture to be economically viable, however, significant international confidence and cooperation is required, as also investment and demand by Japan and Korea.[58]

A key area of friction and a barrier to engagement

between the democratic West and autocratic Beijing is China's relationship with energy-rich rogue states. Chinese companies, backed by political intent and government finances, are willing to invest in countries with high political risk. With competition for scarce energy resources intense, China has pursued deals with international pariah states that are off limits to Western companies because of sanctions, security concerns, or ethical policy and the threat of international condemnation. China's ties with state sponsors of terrorism provide them much-needed resources, allowing these countries to continue to harbour terrorists and to maintain a policy of oppression and exploitation of their people. This highlights the ideological affinity between China and other authoritarian regimes that are also anxious for market transition while maintaining single-party rule – Myanmar, Vietnam, Cambodia, Laos, Iran, Sudan, and North Korea.[59] China remains unconcerned about the source of vital energy, whether Iranian, Kazakh, Sudanese, or Angolan, considering anyone who helps with its oil security problem to be a friend of Beijing. China's unconditional assistance and opaque commercial transactions, which do little to encourage these rogue states to improve their governance systems, are viewed in Beijing as necessary in order to guarantee its own continued economic growth.[60] India, conversely, seems to be aligning itself with the West and is investing significantly in trying to evolve a strategic partnership with the US.

The US, preoccupied with the global war on terrorism, is becoming concerned with Chinese diplomatic activity, particularly in Asia and the Middle East, where its own presence in these regions could be marginalized. China's record of arms sales and support to energy-rich Middle Eastern countries and state sponsors of terrorism in the Gulf region continues to agitate Washington.[61] Asia's oil imports from the Middle East are set to increase rapidly, primarily because of rising demand in China and India and Japan's continuing need to import all of its requirements. Ensuring reliable and stable flows from the Gulf region will be Asia's biggest challenge. This may result in the political and economic dependence of many Middle Eastern states shifting from the West towards Asia. As it is, America's dependence on the Middle East is much less than that of other major global economies as only 17 per cent of its oil imports flow from the region. In fact, it is China that will be importing almost 70 per cent of its oil from the Middle East by 2015.[62]

China will continue to maintain a strong interest in oil production in both Iraq and Iran. These two energy partners are an insurance measure against reduced production from Central Asian oilfields. Iran has explicitly stated its desire for China to replace Japan as the country's largest energy trading partner.[63]

Energy also remains the backbone of the Sino-Saudi relationship. Saudi Arabia is also a major investor in the Chinese refineries. In 1999 Saudi Arabia's Aramco Overseas Company provided a $750 million investment – 25 per cent of the total project cost – in a petrochemical complex in Fujian capable of processing eight million tons of Saudi crude oil per annum. Saudi Arabia, in cooperation with several members of OPEC, intends to build a new refinery in Guangzhou involving a total investment of $8 billion. China is assiduously attempting to enlarge its sphere of influence throughout the Gulf, and its relationship with Saudi Arabia is a key component of this strategy.

China remains concerned over US aspirations to dominate the Middle East in order to secure its own energy requirements while simultaneously containing China's expansion in the region. Some in Beijing, therefore, consider the US as a major threat to China's energy security and remain reluctant to rely on it for the security of their seaborne oil imports, thereby resulting in a focus on developing a blue-water navy to protect its sea lanes of communication.[64] The Iraq war and its aftermath also seem to have reinforced China's fears that it is locked in a zero-sum contest for energy with the US and added urgency to its mission to lessen dependence on Middle Eastern oil supplies. However, if the American predominance of the Middle East weakens and China's profile rises in the region, India's energy security will inevitably be compromised.

INDIA'S LOSS IS CHINA'S GAIN

Indian concerns about Chinese influence across the globe are derived from the perception that it is losing out to China in the energy race. The Chinese have an upper hand over India in bidding, because they can clinch a deal at any cost, while Indian public sector companies need to ensure that the investment provides at least a 12 per cent rate of return. The Chinese companies not only enjoy a head start over their Indian rivals but also have deeper pockets. India is only a recent entrant in the global bidding process, because it was only in 2002 that the government deregulated the domestic oil sector. For China, buying foreign oil and gas fields for energy security has become a central mission, and the Chinese government has allowed its oil majors unprecedented freedom to achieve that goal. China has realized that its energy interests lie in geopolitical relations and has thus decided to focus on these much more intently to address its security needs. And in that pursuit, Chinese oil companies have used all sorts of government aid, including non-oil commitments, transfer of missile technologies, the veto of UN sanctions against countries where China has oil interests, and even education and development aid, to lure energy-rich states.[65] The results are fairly evident.

China, for example, has cemented its ties with Angola, which exported 25 per cent of its output to China in 2001. Angola's future exports are unlikely to decrease after China provided a seventeen-year, $2 billion oil-backed loan in 2005, which the Angolan government is using to rebuild national infrastructure ravaged by years of civil war.[66] According to media reports, although the Indian government also promised a $200 million rail line in Angola (over the $620 million for the oil blocks), the CNPC managed to snatch it away, because the Chinese government offered a composite $2 billion in aid for a variety of projects in Angola.[67] Similarly, China managed to retain its 50 per cent stake in Yadavaran,

Iran, because there was reportedly an informal arrangement for the transfer of missile technology to Iran. A Chinese oil company also won the bid for acquiring the assets of a Canadian oil firm, Encana Corporation, in Ecuador after India decided to withdraw from the deal at the last minute. Even with regard to the much-touted China-India joint bid in Syria, the fact remains that the Syrian fields are not very desirable, with production falling from 390,000 barrels a day in 1995 to about 177,000 barrels per day in 2005. There are enormous political risks in investing in a country such as Syria. China and India seem to have made a practical decision to work together so as to share the risk and to keep the cost of the acquisition down.[68]

While India and China may go in for more overseas bids for foreign energy projects to avoid cut-throat competition, a lasting cooperative arrangement is highly unlikely. China is already way ahead of India in this process, and while it may try to assuage some Indian concerns by partnering with it on projects such as the Syrian one, it is unlikely to gain much from the collaboration. It is India that needs to cooperate with China, rather than the other way around, because it is difficult for India to win over China when they bid for assets. Given that the Chinese are much larger participants in the global oil market, it is not clear what advantages they would derive from cooperation. Where the ONGC spent around $2.1 billion in 2009 acquiring energy and resource assets around the world, state-owned Chinese companies spent as much as $3.2 billion.[69] Moreover, the Indian government's energy strategy still lacks clarity and bureaucratic problems remain endemic. This was reflected in the manner in which the government decided to reject at the last minute the ONGC's apparently winning bid for an up to $2 billion stake in a Nigerian oilfield, thereby damaging the credibility of Indian companies in the international market.[70] In the long term, Chinese companies may see more gain in forming ventures with experienced majors like BP, Royal Dutch Shell, and Exxon Mobil Corporation as compared to teaming with their Indian counterparts.

The fear of lagging behind China in its quest for global influence is forcing India to shape up. But in many ways it is already too late. Despite India's longstanding cultural and commercial ties with Africa, it now finds itself trailing China as it ignored the continent during the 1990s. New Delhi has been tardy in seizing new opportunities in Africa and capitalizing on its long history of engagement with the continent. The UPA government's failure to secure backing of African nations for India's membership in the UN Security Council jolted the government out of its slumber, galvanizing it to strengthen its ties with a continent that has often complained of indifference on the part of New Delhi. China nudged the African Union into taking a position that demanded not only a permanent representation in the Security Council but also veto power. This led to the collapse of the nascent attempts to expand the council.[71]

It is likely that China will seek to preserve and enhance its global economic and political profile further. China is the most likely challenger to US global supremacy and is already using its considerable resources to expand its sphere of influence, from South America to Central Asia, from East Asia to Africa. Its energy diplomacy is also being used towards that end. While it is increasingly challenging US predominance, India is being forced to respond to China's influence in South Asia and beyond. But in the absence of an overarching China policy, India's tentative attempts at managing its rise are bound to fail.

5

INDIA'S CHINA PROBLEM: WHY THE LACK OF A SERIOUS RESPONSE

IN NOVEMBER 2007, the Cabinet Secretary of India sent a note to all the ministers of his government advising them against attending a function organized by, of all organizations, the Gandhi Peace Foundation to felicitate the Dalai Lama.[1] One can think of any number of reasons for this response from the Indian government. The prime minister may have wanted to assuage the concerns of the communist parties, supporting his government from outside, that the foreign policy was tilting towards Washington and so may have signalled that India was keen on preserving the upward trajectory in Sino-Indian ties. It is also possible that the government wanted to thank China for the successful visit of Congress party president Sonia Gandhi to the Middle Kingdom a few days earlier, during which some media reports suggested that China seemed to be taking a more favourable view of the US-India nuclear deal.

The problem was that to most outside observers it was not clear what the government was actually trying to achieve. Its behaviour seemed to contravene India's long-held position on the Dalai Lama's presence in the country, as articulated by none other than Jawaharlal Nehru, that viewed the Dalai Lama as a spiritual leader widely revered in India, much more than a mere political dissident. Moreover, it is debatable if India's genuflection to Chinese concerns on Tibet by ostracizing the Dalai Lama was even in its national interest. The government's position neither lived up to the ideals that India often claims it stands for nor did it clearly enhance India's strategic interests with regard to China. India failed to score on either side of the intellectual divide: realism versus idealism. Later, when the Chinese authorities cracked down on the Tibetan protests in Lhasa and elsewhere during the Olympic torch relay, the Indian government could only express distress at the plight of the Tibetans without condemning the Chinese behaviour.[2] For the Indian government, it seemed a tough balancing act, but for the rest of the world it was a passive foreign policy posture by a state that wants to be recognized as a major global power.

These episodes are symptomatic of the fundamental crisis facing Indian foreign policy at the beginning of this new millennium. As India's weight has grown in the international system in recent years, there's a perception that it is on the cusp of achieving 'great power' status. It is repeated ad nauseam in the domestic and often in global media, and India is already being asked to behave like one. There is just one problem: Indian policy makers themselves are not clear as to what this status of a great power entails. This intellectual vacuum has allowed its foreign policy to drift without any sense of direction, and the result is that as the world looks to India to shape the emerging international order, India has little to offer except some platitudinous rhetoric that does great disservice to its stature. Nowhere are the consequences of such a drift more palpable than in India's engagement with China.

What the discussion in previous chapters of the divergence and convergence of Sino-Indian interests reveals is China's success in attaining its foreign policy objectives and India's failure to preserve its vital interests.

In contrast to China's well-laid-out policy towards India, India has from time to time oscillated from going ballistic over China to a sort of defeatist acquiescence, in the process failing spectacularly in evolving a coherent long-term strategy towards its most important neighbour. This is despite the fact that most serious analyses of Sino-Indian relations indicate the inevitability of a competitive rivalry between the two nations, which should alert Indian decision makers to the need for a strategic approach towards China. Whether India likes it or not, the competition for regional influence will always underpin the realities of the Sino-Indian relationship, and India needs to shape its foreign policy accordingly. It might then seem puzzling that a nation, such as India, that hopes to be a major global player, is so insouciant about its closest competitor. There are, however, important reasons for this lackadaisical Indian approach.

Constraints

There are a number of constraints that impede the development of a clear-eyed China policy in India. Some of these constraints reflect on the larger process of Indian foreign policy-making, while the others are China-specific.

Strategic Culture: Scholars of international politics have time and again focused on culture as an important variable determining state behaviour in the international realm. Culture can refer both to a set of evaluative standards, such as norms or values, and to cognitive standards, such as rules or models defining what entities and actors exist in a system and how they operate and interrelate.[3] It has been argued that the cultural environment affects not only the incentives for different kinds of state behaviour but also how states perceive themselves, what is called a state identity.[4] The cultural elements of a state's domestic environment thereby become an important factor shaping its security interests and security policies.

While critics have argued that culture does not matter in global politics and foreign policy, and that cultural effects can be reduced to epiphenomena (secondary) of the distribution of power and capabilities, one can surely examine culture as one of the variables shaping a state's foreign policy, even if there are reasons to be cautious about using culture to explain political outcomes.

Alastair Iain Johnston argues that China has historically exhibited a relatively consistent hard realpolitik strategic culture that continues even now when, according to him, China faces a threat environment that is the most benign in several decades.[5] China's strategic behaviour exhibits a preference for offensive uses of force, mediated by a keen sensitivity to relative capabilities, and Chinese decision makers seem to have internalized this strategic culture. Johnston has also noted that Chinese decision makers tend to see territorial disputes as high-value conflicts, due in part to a historical sensitivity to threats to the territorial integrity of the state.[6] This is something of direct consequence for the future of Sino-Indian relations. This strategic culture provides Chinese decision makers a set of clear principles as well as a long-term orientation in designing their foreign policy.

Andrew Scobell argues that China's foreign policy and its tendency to use military force are influenced not only by elite understandings of China's own strategic tradition but also by their understanding of the strategic cultures of other states.[7] In this respect, it is important to recognize that Chinese strategists continue to consider India as a militaristic, unstable, and threatening power, with an ambition of separating Tibet from China. In their view, India seeks to dominate its neighbours and foment conflict between China and other nations.[8] This puts India in the category of Chinese rivals along with the US and Japan, states that according to Chinese strategic elites have menacing designs on China's sovereignty and security.

On the other hand, India's ability to think strategically

on issues of national security is at best questionable. George Tanham, in his landmark and controversial study on this subject, points out that Indian elites have shown little evidence of having thought coherently and systematically about national strategy. He argues that this lack of long-term planning and strategy owes largely to India's historical and cultural developmental patterns. These include the Hindu view of life as largely unknowable, thereby being outside man's control, and the Hindu concept of time as eternal, thereby discouraging planning. As a consequence, Tanham argues, India has been on the strategic defensive throughout its history, reluctant to assert itself except within the subcontinent.[9]

India's former Minister for External Affairs, Jaswant Singh, has also examined the evolution of strategic culture in Indian society and in its political decision-making class, with a particular reference to post-independence India. He also finds Indian political elites lacking in the ability to think strategically about foreign policy and defence issues, but he trains his guns on India's first prime minister, Jawaharlal Nehru, pointing to his 'idealistic romanticism' and his unwillingness to institutionalize strategic thinking, policy formulation and implementation.[10]

It is ironical, however, that even when Jaswant Singh was the external affairs minister, there is little evidence that anything of substance really changed in so far as India's China policy is concerned. For all the blame that Singh lays at Nehru's doorsteps, even he and his government did not move towards the institutionalization of strategic thinking, policy formulation, and implementation. Perhaps, the Indian strategic culture was too powerful a constraint for him to overcome.

Lack of Institutionalization: A major consequence of this absence of any Indian strategic culture worth its name is a perceptible lack of institutionalization of the foreign-policy-making process in India. At its very foundation, Indian democracy is sustained by a range of institutions from the more formal ones of the executive, legislative, and the judiciary to the less formal ones of the broader civil society. It is these institutions that in large measure have allowed Indian democracy to thrive and flourish for more than sixty years now, despite a number of constraints that have led to the failure of democracy in many other societies. However, in the realm of foreign policy, it is the lack of institutionalization that has allowed a drift to set in without any long-term orientation. Some have laid the blame on Nehru for his unwillingness to construct strategic planning architecture because he single-handedly shaped Indian foreign policy during his tenure.[11] But even his successors have failed to pursue institutionalization in a consistent manner. The Bharatiya Janata Party (BJP)-led National Democratic Alliance came to power in 1999 promising that it would establish a National Security Council (NSC) to analyse the military, economic, and political threats to the nation and to advise the government on meeting these challenges effectively.[12]

While it did set up the NSC and defined its role in policy formulation, it neglected the institutionalization of the council and the building up of its capabilities to play the role assigned to it, thereby failing to underpin national security by structural and systematic institutional arrangements. Moreover, as has been pointed out, the way the NSC is structured makes long-term planning impossible, thereby negating the very purpose of its formation, and its effectiveness remains hostage to the weight of the National Security Adviser (NSA) in national politics.[13] When the Congress-led United Progressive Alliance came to power in 2004, it promised that it would make the NSC a professional and effective institution and blamed the NDA for making only cosmetic changes in the institutional arrangements. Yet, it has so far failed to make it work in an optimal manner whereby the NSC anticipates national security threats, coordinates the management of national security, and engenders long-term planning by generating new and bold ideas. Important national security decisions are still taken in an ad hoc manner without utilizing the Cabinet Committee on Security, the Strategic Policy Group (comprising key secretaries, service chiefs, and heads of intelligence agencies), and officials of the National Security Advisory Board. The NSA continues to be the most powerful authority on national security, sidelining the institution of the NSC. In the true Indian tradition, personalities continue to trump institutions.

An effective foreign policy institutional framework would not only identify the challenges but also develop a coherent strategy to deal with them, organize and motivate the bureaucracy, and persuade and inform the public. The NSC, by itself, is not a panacea, particularly in light of the inability of the NSC in the US to successfully mediate in the bureaucratic wars and effectively coordinate policy. But the lack of an effective NSC in India is reflective of India's ad hoc decision-making process in the realm of foreign policy, with the result that not once in more than six decades has India produced a national security strategy document.

It is often assumed that India has the necessary institutional wherewithal to translate its growing economic and military capabilities into global influence, even though the Indian state continues to suffer from weak administrative capacity in most areas of policy-making. India cannot emerge as a global power or even a regional one unless it designs appropriate institutions to manage its national assets concomitant to its vision of itself as a major player.

On foreign policy and national security issues, state institutions often do not work because the governments of the day do not want them to work. The fundamental problem remains one where those holding the levers of power succumb to the temptation of controlling institutions and awarding loyalists with assignments, sidelining merit and competence. The onus is largely on the bureaucracy, which is not organized to think strategically. Moreover, it remains insular, not interested in making use of a wider knowledge base. The foreign and security policy bureaucracy tends to view the role of outsiders with suspicion and have opposed even a consultative relationship for fear of sharing influence and access to the political establishment. Given the rapidity with which the international environment has been evolving, the Indian bureaucracy often finds itself out of tune with the changing realities in the realm of foreign policy. More often than not, it tends to perpetuate the status quo by focusing exclusively on responding to events as and when they occur as opposed to conceptualizing at a strategic level.

It is equally the case that a wider culture of non-governmental academics and think tanks is largely absent. India's higher education system remains weak in producing the kind of output that would enhance the country's ability to project itself and its values on the global stage more potently.[14] The issue for India is: Can there be an institutionalized apparatus within a state if there is a lack of sophisticated academic and media discourse outside the state? The broader decimation of Indian academia has had immense consequences for what the state can do by way of institutionalization. India has only a handful of China scholars, most of whom don't even know the Chinese language, and the media is fond of using clichés when dealing with China-related issues. The result: India doesn't really understand China, its problems and its priorities. China is a complicated country and India has no clue as to how it really works. To understand more clearly the implications of China's rise for India, it is important to understand China more deeply. India's scattered and insular foreign policy and national security apparatus have found it difficult to deal with China's top-down, disciplined and aggressive policy machinery.

This lack of effective institutionalization of policy-making has made it difficult for India to assess the implications of a rising China in its neighbourhood with the seriousness that it deserves. In the absence of an effective strategic planning architecture, India's China debate has remained just that, a debate, with no attempt at the highest echelons of foreign policy-making to evolve a coherent strategy towards its neighbour.

India's China Debate: The Indian political establishment is fond of arguing that there is a distinct continuity that defines the country's foreign policy. One can relate this easily to the standard structural-realist theory of international politics, according to which states fashion their foreign policies in response to the systemic constraints imposed by the international system, and domestic politics is not an important variable in this process.[15] In a certain sense, this holds true for Indian foreign policy in general. There have been relatively few dramatic shifts in the policy over the years and these shifts have been engendered by larger systemic forces, such as the end of the Cold War and the disappearance of the Soviet Union.

In so far as India's China policy is concerned, it is true that one does find a certain continuity in the official position. There is a consensus across the political spectrum for improving bilateral ties with China and for resolving Sino-Indian differences through dialogue.[16] However, this official policy hides a broader debate in India about how to deal with China. It has been pointed out that there are three broad groups who hold definite views on this and they have been classified as the pragmatists, the hyper-realists, and the appeasers.[17] The pragmatists view

China as a long-term threat and as a competitor but argue that this competition can be managed by engaging China economically and balancing against it by emerging as a major power in the international system. The hyper-realists view China as a clear and present danger and would like India to contain it by forging alliances around China's periphery and by strengthening India's military capabilities. The appeasers view China as a friendly and benevolent neighbour and would like India to engage that country wholeheartedly as China, in their opinion, is not a threat to India in any way.

Along similar lines, Steven Hoffman has also delineated Indian perceptual positions on China.[18] He has outlined three ideal types which he classifies as the mainstream position, China-Is-Not-Hostile position, and China-Is-Hostile position. These ideal types closely correlate with the pragmatists, the appeasers, and the hyper-realists of the above-mentioned typology. The mainstream Indian perspective on China, according to Hoffman, views China as a potential threat to Indian security but hopes that effective Indian diplomacy can avert any major problems. The China-Is-Not-Hostile perspective holds that China is a rational and peace-loving state that does not have malevolent intentions towards India. In marked contrast, the China-Is-Hostile position views it as a short- and long-term strategic rival and calls for Indian diplomatic assertiveness towards China.

This debate has been going on for quite some time in India. Though this cacophony of views reflects Indian democracy at its best, in many ways it also impedes the formulation of a long-term strategy. The consequence is that the government, realizing that there are a plethora of views on China, has taken the path of least resistance, a policy that keeps most groups satisfied, if not happy, even though it is a policy only in name.

Not surprisingly, the government continues to speak in multiple voices on China. India's environment minister, Jairam Ramesh, could go to Beijing and accuse his own government of being 'overly defensive and alarmist' in dealing with Chinese companies. According to him, the warming of ties between China and India as a consequence of their collaboration on global climate change negotiations was being harmed by the 'suspicious attitude' of the Indian security establishment.[19] He challenged his own government's policy on a foreign soil, in essence suggesting that the Chinese government is right when it underscores time and again that India, not China, is responsible for the recent downward spiral in Sino-Indian ties.

Meanwhile, China has been successful in leveraging its influence in Indian politics to further its agenda. Just as China used the Indian communists to discredit Nehru by portraying him as pro-US, it continues to rely on its ideological brethren to further their cause in India. On a number of issues, the Left parties in India and the CPM in particular have positions which are closely aligned with Chinese positions. Important segments of the media continue to propagate the Chinese narrative on major issues of significance to India, thereby undermining the credibility of Indian positions. Unlike Beijing, New Delhi remains reluctant to take advantage of the many fault lines in Greater China, even though

China's inability to respect ethnic differences within its borders is its Achilles heel.

Power Matters: The success and failure of a nation's foreign policy is largely a function of its power and the manner in which that power is wielded. A state's power in the international system can be defined as a function of the material capabilities that a state possesses. Despite all the talk of India as a rising power, on all indicators of power, economic and military, India remains behind China in terms of its capabilities. While India's economic and military capabilities have no doubt increased substantially in recent times, with its GDP fourth in the world in purchasing power parity and its military the third largest in the world, China's capabilities have continued to trump India's.[20] There is hardly any comparison between India and China at the moment. More important, China is relishing its role as a new global power and is playing it well. For all its rhetoric about the democratization of international affairs, it has steadfastly refused to share its status on the UN Security Council as the sole Asian power.

A fundamental quandary that has long dogged India in the realm of foreign affairs and that has become even more acute with India's ascent in the international order is what Sunil Khilnani has referred to as India's lack of an 'instinct for power'. Unlike China, India is not at ease with the notion of exercising global power. But power, and its pursuit, lies at the heart of international politics. It affects the influence that states exert over one another, thereby shaping political outcomes. The exercise of power can be shocking and at times corrupting, but power is absolutely necessary to fight the battles that must be fought. India's ambivalence about power and its use has resulted in a situation where even as India's economic and military capabilities have gradually expanded, it has failed to evolve a commensurate strategic agenda and requisite institutions so as to be able to mobilize and use its resources most optimally.

Hans J. Morgenthau has written, 'The prestige of a nation is its reputation for power. That reputation, the reflection of the reality of power in the mind of the observers, can be as important as the reality of power itself. What others think about us is as important as what we actually are.'[21] India faces a unique conundrum: its political elites desperately want global recognition for India as a major power and all the prestige and authority associated with that. Yet, they continue to be reticent about the acquisition and use of power in foreign affairs. Most recently, this ambivalence was expressed by the former minister of commerce, Kamal Nath, in a speech when he suggested that 'this word power often makes me uncomfortable'.[22] Though he was talking about the economic rise of India and the challenges that the country continues to face as it strives for sustained economic growth, his discomfort with the notion of India as a rising power was indicative of a larger reality in Indian polity.

This ambivalence about the use of power in international relations, where 'any prestige or authority eventually rely upon traditional measures of power, whether military or economic',[23] is curious as the Indian political elites have rarely shied away from the maximization of power in the realm of domestic politics, thereby corroding the institutional fabric of liberal democracy in the country.

In what has been diagnosed as a 'mini state syndrome', those states which do not have the material capabilities to make a difference to outcomes at the international level often denounce the concept of power in foreign policy-making.[24] India had long been a part of such states, viewing itself as an object of the foreign policies of a small majority of powerful nations. As a consequence, the political and strategic elites developed a suspicion of power politics with the word power itself acquiring a pejorative connotation in so far as foreign policy was concerned. The relationship between power and foreign policy was never fully understood, leading to a progressive loss in India's ability to wield power effectively in the international realm. Today, when India wants to shape the international system as opposed to being merely its referent object, it is more important than ever that its foreign policy is 'anchored on a planned augmentation of the power of the nation as a whole'.[25] Even the pious declarations of world peace, disarmament and global development that India continues to propound on the world stage will be taken seriously if they come from a nation that the international community perceives has the will and the ability to convert its rhetoric into reality. Put simply, even the rhetoric of powerful nations matters.

A nation's vital interests, in the ultimate analysis, can only be preserved and enhanced if it has sufficient power capabilities at its disposal. But not only must a nation possess such capabilities, there must also be a willingness to employ the required forms of power in pursuit of those interests. India's lack of an instinct for power is most palpable in the realm of the military, where unlike other major global powers of the past and the present India has failed to master the creation, deployment and use of its military instruments in support of its national objectives.[26] Nehru envisioned making India a global leader without any help from the nation's armed forces, arguing, 'the right approach to defence is to avoid having unfriendly relations with other countries – to put it differently, war today is, and ought to be, out of question'.[27] War has been systematically factored out of Indian foreign policy and the national security matrix, with the resulting ambiguity about India's ability to withstand major wars of the future. The modern state system, in fact the very nature of the state itself, has been determined to a significant degree by the changing demands of war, and it has developed through a series of what Philip Bobbitt has called 'Epochal Wars'.[28] A defining feature of any state is its ability to make war and keep peace.

Military power, more often than not, affects the success with which other instruments of statecraft are employed, as it always lurks in the background of inter-state relations, even when nations are at peace with each other. It remains central to the course of international politics as force retains its role as the final arbiter among states in an anarchical international system.[29] States may not always need to resort to the actual use of force, but military power vitally affects the manner in which states deal with each other even during peace time, despite what the protagonists of globalization and liberal institutionalism might claim. A state's diplomatic posture will lack effectiveness if it is not backed by a credible military posture.

Few nations face the kind of security challenges that confront India. Yet, since independence the military was never seen as a central instrument in the achievement of national priorities, the tendency of the political elites being to downplay the importance of military power. India ignored the defence sector after independence and paid inadequate attention to its defence needs. Even though the policy makers themselves had little knowledge of critical defence issues, the armed forces had little or no role in the formulation of defence policy till 1962.[30] Divorcing foreign policy from military power was a recipe for disaster, as India realized in 1962, when even Nehru was forced to concede that 'military weakness has been a temptation, and a little military strength may be a deterrent'.[31] A state's legitimacy is tied to its ability to monopolize the use of force and operate effectively in an international strategic environment, and India had lacked clarity on this relationship between the use of force and its foreign policy priorities.

India is yet to learn the ability 'to integrate the creation, deployment and use of military instruments in support of national objectives'.[32] In stark contrast to India, China has shown a willingness to use force quite readily in pursuit of its national goals, while always insisting that it is defensive in nature. Chinese leaders tend to rationalize even their offensive military operations as purely defensive and measures of last resort (this logic has also been applied to the 1962 Sino-India war), to an extent where defence can even include a pre-emptive strike.[33]

Indian foreign policy's failure to achieve its objectives in respect of China has a lot to do with its as yet underdeveloped power capabilities. On the other hand, China's rising power and the effectiveness with which it has wielded it has allowed that country to achieve most of its strategic objectives with regard to India. While Indians keep coining nonsensical terms like 'Chindia', few Chinese take such ideas seriously.[34] In fact, China does not even consider India as worthy of being its rival. As Susan Shirk points out, 'Underlying China's relaxed attitude towards India is its confidence, verging on arrogance, about Chinese capabilities and its low opinion of Indian capabilities.'[35]

Power matters and, in international politics, weakness begets failure while strength begets strategic clout. India overdoes restraint, partly because of real constraints but mostly because its policy makers can't really make up their minds about the use of power in foreign policy. There's a reason why major powers tend to flex their muscles. Unless India achieves higher rates of economic growth and modernizes its military, both quantitatively and qualitatively, and learns to use its military instruments in pursuit of national objectives, its foreign policy will struggle to achieve the results it desires.

Outcome

As a consequence of various constraints that have impeded the evolution of a long-term China policy in India, India's approach towards China remains ambivalent, shifting from bombastic jingoism to defeatist acquiescence with dangerous alacrity. This lack of direction in policy is clearly revealed by the manner in which it has dealt with China in the past few years. While Sino-Indian bilateral relations have apparently improved, it is not clear if India has any idea as to what ends it wants to harness this improvement and what its strategic objectives with respect to China are. This has resulted in foreign policy flip-flops doing much damage to India's regional and global diplomatic stature. Of course, even muddling through can be viewed as a strategic choice, but it is rarely the smartest one.

A former defence minister, George Fernandes, described China as India's 'enemy number one' and a former prime minister, Atal Bihari Vajpayee, wrote to the US that the Indian nuclear tests were a response to the threat posed by China. But some five years later, China became a 'good neighbour' for the same Indian government when the prime minister visited Beijing. What brought about this remarkable transformation, of course, remains absolutely unclear till date. The Manmohan Singh government came to office declaring that it wants to have friendly relations with China, which, of course, is a reasonable foreign policy objective. But without a clear articulation of India's national security objectives, such declarations remain just pious rhetoric and rhetoric has never been in short supply in Sino-Indian relations. Without any hint of irony, Manmohan Singh can suggest that China is India's 'greatest neighbour'. Pursuit of friendly relations with China seems to have become an end in itself when it should be a means towards achieving India's larger strategic objective of emerging as a major regional and global player.

The China policy is in many ways symptomatic of a larger misunderstanding in the Indian political establishment with regard to what a nation's foreign policy should be. For the left-liberal strand in the Indian polity, foreign policy is merely an extension of domestic policy. As such, since India is a secular, democratic, and peace-loving nation, its pursuit of its relations with other states should merely be a reflection of these virtues. This has given rise to much of the moral rhetoric in foreign affairs that India has been spouting for the better part of the last sixty years and which still continues to shape the understanding of global politics of major political formations on the left of the Indian political spectrum. The discourse, in the words of one of the most astute observers of Indian foreign policy, 'has remained frozen in a rhetorical trap, reminiscent of our class X essays in the earnest, third-worldist, allegedly non-aligned seventies'.[36] A vivid example of this attitude is the rather extreme positions on national security taken by the communist parties consistently. While emphasizing their fraternal ties with China's Communist Party time and again, they have called for an end to all military cooperation with the US, asking the government to return to a policy of 'genuine non-alignment'. They remain completely silent on Chinese activities adversely affecting Indian national security interests, even as they show no compunction in vociferously denouncing the US as a global imperialist.[37]

Manmohan Singh himself has articulated a vision of Indian foreign policy, according to which foreign policy exists to push pragmatic economic goals, especially as India integrates more and more with the global economy, and also to build a world of open, inclusive nations. This understanding of foreign policy unambiguously identifies India with other liberal democracies of the world. The prime minister also suggested that the global environment had never been more conducive for India's economic development than it was today and the world wanted to help India to achieve its full potential. He argued that India should engage other great powers such as the US and China to the fullest and neither should be treated as an adversary.[38] While there is much to commend in this articulation of the Indian foreign policy agenda, particularly the exhortation that India should rise and take full advantage of the opportunities presented by the changing global economic milieu, it is rather naïve in its assertion that foreign policy is nothing more than an outcome of economic policy and that international politics is nothing but a sum total of global trade and economic cooperation.

It is in fact an offshoot of that liberal fallacy that assumes that only if nations trade with each other more, the world would become more prosperous and peaceful. In the case of Sino-Indian relations, many have argued that once economics becomes the driving factor, it will usher in a 'paradigm shift' in Sino-Indian bilateral relations.[39] Major future problems can, therefore, be averted by embedding Sino-Indian relations within a context of expanding economic ties. In many ways, this has become the dominant narrative of Sino-Indian relations in recent years.

K. Subrahmanyam has argued that China's desire for increasing its bilateral trade with India and collaboration in sectors such as information technology can be effectively leveraged in shaping its attitudes towards India.[40] In a recent study, Jairam Ramesh, an influential member of the ruling Congress party, has come up with the concept of 'ChindiA' that denotes synergy between the two. He views closer economic cooperation between China and India as the best way to build trust and friendship, leading to a long-lasting peace between the two states.[41]

The problem with these assumptions is that not only is there little empirical evidence to prove that more trade leads to peace and tranquillity, but also that while politics and economics are certainly interrelated, the international economic system rests upon international political order and not vice versa. Indian foreign policy cannot be conducted on the naïve assumption that greater economic integration with the world would somehow solve all its foreign policy problems.

On the other hand, the Indian right, because of its preoccupation with establishing a 'Hindu' nation and minority-bashing, has extended its narrow sectarian view to foreign policy. The consequence has been its obsession with Pakistan as evil incarnate in its foreign policy agenda and its inclination to view the world in black and white, friends and enemies, evil and noble. While undoubtedly pursuing pragmatic economic and foreign policies when in power, the Indian right, as represented by the BJP, remains under tremendous pressure to revert back to its extremist views once out of power. Where multiculturalism and pluralism should be leveraged as India's strengths in negotiating with an increasingly polarized outside world, the right, with its resistance to India's plural heritage, has been more interested in turning the country into a mirror image of Pakistan.

And then there is the great Indian foreign policy bureaucracy which suffers from the same myopia that Henry Kissinger long back diagnosed for the US foreign service, in that it views its role as merely a negotiating instrument and a solver of concrete issues as they come about, rather than one of shaping events and conceptualizing strategy.

Shaped by these forces, Indian foreign policy has merely been one of responding to events around it rather than anticipating them and evolving coherent long-term strategies to deal with them in the best interests of the country. Every nation needs a long-term strategy that is more than a mere delineation of its interests, where all the different elements of power can be placed in relation to the concrete circumstances of that country, not in relation to abstract ideals. The greatest casualty of this larger foreign policy malaise has been India's China policy. From *Hindi-Chini bhai-bhai* to enemy number one to a great friend, India just does not know how to deal with its neighbourhood dragon. Surely alarmism is not a policy, but neither is hope.

TACKLING CHINA

India has no option but to address the rise of China more purposefully at multiple levels.

First of all, it is imperative that Indian policy makers recognize the true extent of the challenge posed by China to Indian interests. India tends to sweep under the carpet real bilateral problems even as it remains eager to show off examples of Sino-Indian global partnership on various issues. Despite all evidence to the contrary, India continues to emphasize that the two sides have made 'considerable progress' on the boundary issues with China and tends to hold so-called 'vested interests' responsible for problems in Sino-Indian relations.[42] Notwithstanding China's concerted and unambiguous attempts at curtailing India's rise and ensuring that there remains a strategic parity between India and Pakistan, India's national security advisor, Shiv Shankar Menon, could go to Beijing and suggest that China and India 'are no longer in an either-or, zero-sum game kind of situation'. He went on to argue that India's relationship with China 'is not dependent on the state of our [India's] relations with Pakistan, or vice versa. And judging by what we [Indians] have seen in practice over the last few years. I think that is also true of China.'[43] This was an extraordinary statement given that Menon apparently also raised the issue of

China's proposed sale of nuclear reactors to Pakistan during the same visit. It is worth asking what Menon has been observing in China's practice over the last few years that others have failed to notice. The potential of even a limited Sino-Indian partnership cannot be realized if such blatant political hypocrisy continues.

It has been noted even by non-Indian observers that the Indian strategic discourse tends to overemphasize the promising future potentials in Sino-Indian relationship and de-emphasize troublesome past and present realities. However, a stable foundation for the future of Sino-Indian relations cannot be laid by feigning total ignorance of Chinese activities that have adversely affected Indian national interests in the past. India needs to be upfront about the lack of progress in finding mutually acceptable territorial concessions.

Pranab Mukherjee, as external affairs minister, had suggested that 'we [Indians] would need to develop more sophisticated ways of dealing with these new challenges posed by China . . . as China seeks to further her interests more aggressively than in the past'.[44] Of course, by now the Indian government should have done more to set the priorities, bring ends and means into better balance and acquaint the Indian public with some uncomfortable realities about Sino-Indian ties. Yet, being the quintessential argumentative nation, it is talking that India does best while China can go ahead and accomplish the tasks at hand, because the Indian political leadership has become apathetic on this issue. It doesn't help when Indian policy makers continue to console themselves that there are no Chinese bases in the Indian Ocean at a time when the Chinese thinkers are openly suggesting that establishing bases overseas is a Chinese right.[45] Therefore, the sooner the Indian policy makers regain their nerve the better, because the next few years aren't going to be easy.

Second, India has to put its own house in order and focus on redressing the balance of power with China. It needs to develop its economic and military might without in any way being apologetic about it. It needs to clearly articulate its national interests and engage China on a host of issues, from the border problem to the alleged dumping of cheap Chinese goods in the Indian market. India needs to recognize that appeasing China is neither desirable nor necessary, even as a direct confrontation with China is not something India can afford, at least in the near future.

Indian policy makers should start acknowledging the real driver behind China's policies. Rather than debating if China is a malevolent or a benevolent power, India should realize that it is the structure of global politics that by definition makes Sino-Indian competition inevitable. There are only two options for India – either play the game of global politics by the rules laid down by its structure or resign itself to a secondary status in the global hierarchy. Given that Indian decision makers already talk of India as a global player in the making, they cannot but take the rules of the game that is global politics seriously. Of course, a Sino-Indian competition that can be diplomatically managed would be in everyone's interest. But historically, rising powers have tried to reshape their strategic environment to reflect new realities of power and this has provoked conflicts. The idea — that many in India share — that only if India provokes China would it threaten India is fundamentally flawed. Given the rapidity of China's rise, it is beyond Indian hands to shape the future of Sino-Indian relations. China will react to its own strategic environment and if it finds that it is not commensurate with its rising prowess, it will get provoked. India's weakness, in that case, would do more harm than good.

India, therefore, should start playing the balance of power game more seriously. It should learn from China, which has mastered this art to perfection. Given the growing disparity between the two, India needs the US as an offshore balancer in the region to prevent China from gaining regional hegemony. A close US-India relationship, warts and all, is the only option available to India in the short to medium term. But given the relative economic decline of the US, it too needs more allies in the region to balance China's growing might. And to underscore India's utility in the emerging strategic milieu, it should signal clearly that Washington cannot take India's support for granted. Meanwhile, India needs a more pro-active Asia-Pacific policy that involves greater engagement with states on China's periphery such as Japan, Vietnam, Taiwan, and Indonesia. India will have to emerge as a credible balancer in the region, otherwise states in the Asia-Pacific will end up joining the Chinese bandwagon. India's diffidence in power projection is creating a perception in the region that there's nothing to fear from New Delhi and everything to gain by ingratiating with India's adversary,

China. To prevent such an eventuality, India should be seen as ready and willing to look after its interests purposefully and efficiently.

India should also attempt a more rigorous internal balancing posture vis-à-vis China. Again, New Delhi has much to learn from Beijing in building its military profile. Good fences make for good neighbours. India's defences should be strong and secure irrespective of what China does or doesn't do. India must play to its strengths and should resist the temptation to match China weapon for weapon. Even as China continues to pursue its national security objectives through careful defence planning and expenditure, Indian defence planning remains ad hoc in nature with no clearly defined end-state. The real issue in India's case is effective management of available budgetary resources, because a developing, democratic country like India will always be constrained in what it can spend on defence. While a major portion of the military budget continues to go towards revenue expenditure, India continues to lag behind in investing in research and development – which means it continues to rely on other countries for cutting-edge technologies, thereby perpetuating the vicious cycle. This is mainly because India doesn't have a coherent national security strategy that maps out its long-term challenges along with concomitant defence planning. Effective defence planning and force structuring require a coherent grand strategy and an appropriate institutional framework, something that India has somehow never found the will to develop. It is here, rather than in matching defence expenditure figure by figure, that India should try to emulate China.

Third, India should stop talking about becoming a global leader. No one takes such claims seriously when India has been unable to get a grip on its own neighbourhood. Only after India becomes a net provider of regional security can it expect its power projection beyond its shores to have any real significance. Using *sama, dama, danda, bhed,* India should establish its hegemony in its periphery. If China can so easily penetrate India's immediate neighbourhood – its first ring of defence – what hope does India have of competing with China in the far-flung regions of the world? India should use its rise as an economic power to create a web of economic interdependence in South Asia, something that it has been lackadaisical about. India remains overly cautious in offering market access to its neighbours, while China has successfully leveraged its economic might from South Asia and East Asia to Africa and Latin America.

India's structural dominance in South Asia makes it a natural target of resentment among its smaller neighbours. And therefore most of these states have sought to balance Indian influence by courting China. India's challenge is twofold: First, it must engage its neighbours in a productive manner that will allow it to realize its dream of emerging as a global power. Second, it must prevent China from gaining a strategic foothold in South Asia and preserve its influence in the region. Yet, for all the talk of India as a rising power, New Delhi has found it difficult to emerge as a leader in its own backyard. By being risk averse and not proactive, it has ceded the strategic space in the region to China.

Fourth, India should cease being defensive. India walks on shells for fear of offending China, while China has had no such compunction. India should have the self-confidence to stand up to China. And the first step in this direction would be to make the contents of the Henderson Brooks–P.S. Bhagat report of the 1962 war debacle public. The humiliation of 1962 remains embedded in the collective Indian consciousness. India needs to come to terms with itself and its defeat before it can engage China with a measure of confidence. By refusing to declassify the report, the Indian government has allowed the Chinese to propagate their version of history. It has not only prevented the armed forces from learning lessons from a war that has psychologically scarred generations of Indians but has also not allowed India from having an honest debate on China.

A nation's foreign policy is not merely a product of what it wants but also of what other countries do to it. For far too long, India has allowed China to dictate the terms of their mutual engagement. India is expected to explain its every move while China can get away with almost anything. There is no need to kowtow to China's every whim. China, for example, sent a demarche to New Delhi when India conducted naval exercises with the US, Japan and Australia, seeking to know the objective of the quadrilateral initiative. New Delhi, on its part, remains hesitant to engage Taipei even as other states have pursued a pragmatic approach with Taiwan within the rubric of a 'one-China' policy. It was after sixty-five years that the leader of the Chinese Nationalist Party was invited to India in 2007. China cannot be allowed to dictate the terms of India's rise. Whereas India went overboard in making sure that the Olympic torch passed undisturbed, not even allowing peaceful protests by Tibetans, China summoned the Indian ambassador in Beijing past midnight to lodge a protest over the breach of security of its embassy premises in New Delhi.

There is no reason for New Delhi not to be accommodating on trade issues even as it should hold its ground on security issues. India cannot and should not restrict trade and investment from China. After all, China has sought to engage India while at the same time tried to contain it to the best of its abilities. Indian policy makers remain diffident, almost apologetic, about their nation's rising profile. And when they interact with major powers, they reveal this weakness embedded in the Indian psyche. So when the Indian external affairs minister went to Beijing to mark the sixtieth anniversary of India's recognition of the People's Republic of China, he ended up pleading once again for Chinese support for India's permanent membership of the UN Security Council. It is unseemly for a nation that claims to be a rising power beseeching Beijing for its support, only to be rebuffed time and again. More damagingly, it betrays a lack of confidence in India's own ability to define the terms of its rise.

China is not going to support India's candidature for the Security Council, at least not in the foreseeable future. If the Indian foreign policy establishment cannot understand this basic fact of Asian geostrategy, they have no right to be running this nation's foreign policy.

Every time India asks for China's support and gets a negative answer it only underlines China's status as the pre-eminent Asian power that reserves the right to grant India the privilege of being in the Security Council.[46]

Words are important but actions speak louder. In so far as its attitudes towards India are concerned, China's words and actions do not yet cohere. China will take India seriously when India starts taking itself seriously and starts behaving like a major power. China is nothing if not pragmatic in its foreign policy. Its support for India's candidature to the Security Council's permanent membership will come when India's rise becomes a reality that Beijing can no longer ignore. A diffident India will continue to crave for the attention of Beijing but will not get it in return. A confident India that charts its own course in world politics based on its national interests will force the world to sit up and take notice.

The rise of India might be an idea whose time has come but the challenges emanating from a rising China are varied and not amenable to easy solutions. The dithering in New Delhi over how to deal with Beijing's growing assertiveness has led to serious doubts emerging about India's ability to leverage the present economic and strategic opportunities to its advantage. Countering the challenge posed by China is a task requiring a kind of intellectual and ideological agility that India has not yet demonstrated it is capable of. It is up to India now to allay these concerns and take its rightful place in the comity of nations.

India's economic rise in the last few years presented

opportunities that the nation's decision makers have not adequately exploited or leveraged to their nation's advantage. It would indeed be a tragedy if history were to describe today's Indian policy makers in the words Winston Churchill applied to those who ignored the changing strategic realities before the Second World War: 'They go on in strange paradox, decided only to be undecided, resolved to be irresolute, adamant for drift, solid for fluidity, all-powerful to be impotent.' India today, more than any other time in its history, needs a view of its role in the world quite removed from the shibboleths of the past. Drift is no longer a viable alternative.

EPILOGUE

> 'All men can see these tactics whereby I conquer, but what none can see is the strategy out of which victory is evolved.'
>
> —Sun Tzu

AFTER DRAMATICALLY INCREASING its military expenditure over the last several years, China raised it by only 7.5 per cent in 2010, marking the first time in nearly twenty-one years that the rate of increase has fallen below double digits.[1] There are a number of reasons behind this but the Chinese government has used the drop to announce its pacific intent, underlining that it has always tried to limit defence spending to a reasonable level. China's foreign policy thinkers and political establishment have long been trying to convince the world that Beijing's rise is meant to be a peaceful one, that China has no expansionist intentions, and that it will be a different kind of great power.

Of course, the very nature of power makes this largely a charade, but more surprising is that Western liberals have tended to take these assertions at face value. There is an entire industry that would have us believe that China is actually a different kind of a great power and that if the West could simply give China a stake in the established order, Beijing's rise would not create any complications.

In 1974, Deng Xiaoping told the UN General Assembly, 'China is not a superpower, nor will it ever seek to be one.' But that was then. Today's Chinese foreign policy thinkers are advocating the creation of overseas bases by China. Shen Dingli, a professor at Fudan University in Shanghai, asserts that 'it is wrong for us [China] to believe that we have no rights to set up bases abroad'. He argues that it is not terrorism or piracy that's the real threat to China. It's the ability of other states to block China's trade routes that poses the greatest threat. To prevent this from happening, China, according to Dingli, needs not only a blue-water navy but also 'overseas military bases to cut the supply costs'.[2]

Dingli, not surprisingly, also wraps this up in the standard rhetoric of world peace, asserting that the establishment of such military bases overseas would promote regional and global stability. It is a familiar diplomatic wrapping that other superpowers should easily recognize.

As China emerges as a major power, it will expand its military footprint across the globe, much like other great powers throughout history. When the Chinese navy went to tackle piracy off the Somali coast in 2009, it was the first time Beijing was using its navy to escort vessels sailing under its national flag at such a distance from its homeland. Though the Chinese navy is not yet capable of conducting sustained missions far from home, Beijing is no longer coy about its ambition to build a navy commensurate with its rising political and economic profile. As Chinese ships chased out a Japanese survey vessel in the disputed waters of the East China Sea in May 2010, a Chinese general explained: 'We kept silent and tolerant over territorial disputes with our neighbours in the past because our navy was incapable of defending our economic zones, but now the navy is able to carry out its task.'[3]

China's expansionist behaviour has been evident for some time now. China has been acquiring naval bases along the crucial choke points in the Indian Ocean to serve its economic interests and to enhance its strategic presence in the region. It is China's growing dependence on maritime space and resources that is reflected in its aspiration to expand its influence and to ultimately dominate the strategic environment of the Indian Ocean region.

The Chinese navy may be a long way off from being able to operate fully independently at long range to meet a full range of military objectives, but China is investing in new strategic relationships that will help PLAN realize its blue-water ambitions. With strong political and diplomatic ties with countries in the Indian Ocean and by helping them build modern port facilities, China can easily get access to these facilities without actually needing military bases.

Meanwhile, recent suggestions emanating from Beijing that China is likely to set up military bases overseas to counter American influence and exert pressure on India have been interpreted in certain sections in New Delhi as a veiled reference to China's interest in having a permanent military presence in Pakistan. Even though it might not be politically possible for the Pakistani government to openly allow China to set up a military base, New Delhi fears that Islamabad might allow Beijing use of its military facilities without any public announcements about it.[4]

To be sure, China is merely following in the footsteps of other major global powers who have established military bases abroad to secure their interests. There is only one kind of great power, and one kind of great power tradition. China is not going to be any different.

A superpower is a superpower, and it is time to shed the sophomore naivety that has surprisingly upheld the belief that China's ascent to power will be any different: power is necessarily expansionist.

The sooner Indian policy makers acknowledge this, the better it will be for India's interests.

NOTES

1. INTRODUCTION

1. 'China should break up India into 20-30 states: Chinese strategist,' Indo Asian News Service, 10 August 2009.
2. Manu Pubby, 'Indian submarine, Chinese warship test each other in pirate waters,' *Indian Express*, New Delhi, 5 February 2009.
3. Chidanand Rajghatta, 'Chinese deception, Nehru's naivete led to '62 war: CIA papers,' *Times of India*, 27 June 2007.

2. THE SINO–INDIAN CONVERGENCE: BILATERAL AND GLOBAL

1. 'India's new defense chief sees Chinese military threat,' *New York Times*, 5 May 1998, p. A6.
2. The text of the letter was published in the *New York Times*, 13 May 1998, p. A12.
3. The JWG was set up in 1988 during Rajiv Gandhi's visit as prime minister to China to explore the boundary issue and examine probable solutions to the problem. As

a follow-up in 1993, the two sides signed the Agreement on the Maintenance of Peace and Tranquillity along the Line of Actual Control in the India-China Border Areas. Thereafter, the India-China Expert Group of Diplomatic and Military Officials (EG) was set up under the JWG. Both the JWG and EG have been meeting regularly since then.

4. Anil K. Joseph, 'Wen to seek resolution of border dispute,' *Indian Express*, New Delhi, 15 March 2005.
5. For details, see the 'Declaration on Principles for Relations and Comprehensive Cooperation Between the Republic of India and the People's Republic of China,' available at <http://meaindia.nic.in/jdhome.htm>.
6. Amit Baruah, 'China keeps its word on Sikkim,' *Hindu*, Chennai, 7 May 2004.
7. J.N. Dixit, 'A new security framework,' *Telegraph*, Kolkata, 17 May 2004.
8. The text of Prime Minister Manmohan Singh's address to the nation is available at http://www.indianembassy.org/pm/pm_jun_24_04.htm.
9. 'India-Russia-China Axis Hinted at After Kosovo Strikes,' *The Associated Foreign Press*, 28 March 1999. Also, see 'Russia, China, India Pile up Pressure on West over Kosovo,' *Indian Express*, New Delhi, 26 March 1999.
10. James Clad, 'Convergent Chinese and Indian Perspectives on the Global Order,' in Francine R. Frankel and Harry Harding (eds), *The India-China Relationship: What the United States Needs to Know* (New York: Columbia University Press, 2004), p. 285.
11. Ibid., pp. 271–284.
12. Juliet Eilperin, 'US pushes for emissions cuts from China, developing nations,' *Washington Post*, 10 December 2009.

13. K.G. Narendranath, 'Jairam has a Copenhagen axis: India, China, Brazil, South Africa,' *Indian Express*, New Delhi, 8 December 2009.
14. Detailed statistics on the latest global energy trends can be found in International Energy Agency, *World Energy Outlook 2009* (Paris, October 2009), Web site http://www.worldenergyoutlook.org.
15. For statistical details on energy demand and supply, see the 'Statistical Review of World Energy 2006' at http://www.bp.com/productlanding.do?categoryId=91& contentId =7017990.
16. Leonardo Maugeri, *The Age of Oil: The Mythology, History and Future of the World's Most Controversial Resource* (Praeger, 2006).
17. Clifford Krauss, 'Economy and geopolitics decide where oil goes next,' *New York Times*, 4 January 2008.
18. Edward R. Fried and Philip H. Trezise, *Oil Security: Retrospect and Prospect* (Washington, DC: Brookings Institution Press, 1993), p. 1.
19. Erica Downs, 'The Chinese Energy Debate,' *The China Quarterly* (March 2004): pp. 21–22.
20. Ashish Vachhani, 'India's energy security dilemma,' *Hindu Business Line*, Chennai, 26 April 2005.
21. Ibid.
22. This report of the Expert Committee on Integrated Energy Policy is available at http://planningcommission.nic.in/reports/genrep/rep_intengy.pdf.
23. For details on India's changing policies in the energy sector, see http://petroleum.nic.in/.
24. Siddhartha Varadarajan, 'India, China primed for energy cooperation,' *Hindu*, Chennai, 13 January 2006.
25. Pranab Dhal Samanta, 'N-energy, UN: China and India signal friendship, not rivalry,' *Indian Express*, New Delhi, 15 January 2008.

26. Vandana Hari, 'India and China: An Energy Team?' *Business Week*, 6 December 2005.
27. Vikas Dhoot, 'What the Prime Minister wants everyone to read,' *Indian Express*, New Delhi, December 2007.
28. Sujan Chinoy, 'IT makes sense for both,' *Indian Express*, New Delhi, 16 April 2005.
29. S. Laxman, 'China seeks nuclear input from India,' *Times of India*, New Delhi, 13 December 2003.
30. 'China Pursues India-Pakistan Peace,' *Wall Street Journal*, 8 December 2003.
31. Ziad Haider, 'Oil Fuels Beijing's New Power Game,' available at http://yaleglobal.yale.edu/display.article?id=5411
32. Zhang Yan, 'India-China relations in one of the best periods in history,' *Hindu*, Chennai, 9 April 2009.

3. DIVERGING TRAJECTORIES

1. 'For China, one party is enough,' *New York Times*, 16 September 2004.
2. Jim Yardley, 'Chinese leaders are resilient in face of change,' *New York Times*, 7 August 2008.
3. Philip P. Pan, *Out of Mao's Shadow* (New York: Simon & Schuster, 2008).
4. David Shambaugh, China's Communist Party: Atrophy and Adaptation (Washington, DC: Woodrow Wilson Center, 2008).
5. Joseph Kahn, 'China's leader closes door to reform,' *New York Times*, 16 October 2008.
6. John Kamm, 'Blinded by the firewall,' *Washington Post*, 7 August 2007.
7. 'Many Chinese think India greatest security threat after US: new poll,' *Indian Express*, New Delhi, 2 December 2009.

8. Saibal Dasgupta, 'India-China Relations: Rao clears negative perceptions,' *Times of India*, 8 July 2009.
9. 'Fear of the Dragon,' *The Economist*, 11 January 2010.
10. Robert Fogel, '$123, 000, 000, 000, 000,' *Foreign Policy*, January/February 2010.
11. For some of the standard reactions, see http://www.economist.com/World/asia/PrinterFriendly.cfm?Story_ID=1858862.
12. Amit Mitra, 'An unequal relationship,' *Times of India*, New Delhi, 12 January 2008.
13. John Pomfret, 'Google's decision signals change in Western businesses' approach to China,' *Washington Post*, 24 March 2010.
14. Peter Wonacott, 'Downturn heightens China-India tension on trade,' *Wall Street Journal*, 20 March 2009.
15. Ibid.
16. Shishir Gupta, 'Contrary to what Left says, 87% of FDI proposals from Chinese firms cleared,' *Indian Express*, New Delhi, 13 November 2006.
17. Swaminathan S. Anklesaria Aiyar, 'Free Trade Area or Yuan Trap,' *Times of India*, 26 November 2006.
18. See, for example, Simon Long, 'Curry in Hot Garlic Sauce,' *Outlook*, 14 April 2005.
19. See the US Department of Defense 'Annual Report on the Military Power of the People's Republic of China,' at http://www.defenselink.mil/pubs/d20040528PRC.pdf.
20. See the report of an independent task force of the Council on Foreign Relations on Chinese Military Power at http://www.cfr.org/pdf/China_TF.pdf.
21. For details, see http://www.defenselink.mil/pubs/d20040528PRC.pdf.
22. Ravi V. Prasad, 'America's two timing,' *Hindustan Times*, New Delhi, 17 March 2004.

23. The 2008 National Defense White Paper of China is available at http://www.gov.cn/english/official/2009-01/20/content_1210227.htm.
24. Ibid.
25. Bill Gertz, 'China report urges missile shield,' *Washington Times*, 1 October 2008.
26. Ashley J. Tellis, 'China's space weapons,' *Wall Street Journal*, 23 July 2007.
27. John Schwartz, 'When computers attack,' *New York Times*, 24 June 2007.
28. Pranab Dhal Samanta, 'RAW suspects "Chinese connection" between its officer in Colombo and a woman, calls him back,' *Indian Express*, New Delhi, 2 October 2007.
29. Manu Pubby, 'China cyber attack: NIC most affected, 9 embassies hit,' *Indian Express*, New Delhi, 31 March 2009.
30. Ravi Visvesvaraya Prasad, 'The breach in the wall,' *Hindustan Times*, New Delhi, 20 March 2009.
31. Saikat Datta, 'The China Doctrine–II,' *Outlook*, 31 December 2007.
32. Pranab Dhal Samanta, 'The dragon has now got wings,' *Indian Express*, 5 January 2008.
33. Ibid.
34. Anthony H. Cordesman and Martin Kleiber, *The Asian Conventional Military Balance in 2006*, The Centre for Strategic and International Studies, June 2006, p. 32.
35. Robert D. Kaplan, 'Lost at sea,' *New York Times*, 21 September 2007.
36. *The Military Balance*, The International Institute for Strategic Studies, 2008, pp. 360–61.
37. Thomas Kane, *Chinese Grand Strategy and Maritime Power* (London: Frank Cass, 2002), p. 139.
38. Youssef Bodansky, 'The PRC surge for the Strait of

Malacca and Spratly confronts India and the US,' *Defense and Foreign Affairs Strategic Policy*, Washington, DC, 30 September 1995, pp. 6-13.
39. Manu Pubby, 'China's new n-submarine base sets off alarm bells,' *Indian Express*, New Delhi, 3 May 2008.
40. Bill Gertz, 'China builds up strategic sea lanes,' *Washington Times*, 18 January 2005.
41. For a detailed explication of the security ramifications of the Chinese 'string of pearls' strategy, see Gurpreet Khurana, 'China's "String of Pearls" in the Indian Ocean and Its Security Implications,' *Strategic Analysis*, Vol. 32, No. 1 (January 2008), pp. 1-22.
42. For a nuanced analysis of this, see Andrew Selth, 'Chinese Military Bases in Burma: The Explosion of a Myth,' Griffith Asia Institute, Regional Outlook Paper No. 10, 2007.
43. Ziad Haider, 'Oil Fuels Beijing's new Power Game,' Yale Global Online, available at http://yaleglobal.yale.edu/display.article?id=5411.
44. Geoffrey Till, *Seapower: A Guide for the Twenty-First Century* (London: Frank Cass, 2004), p. 102.
45. 'China against India, Pakistan joining nuclear club,' *Hindu*, Chennai, 30 June 2004.
46. Andrew Scobell, *China and Strategic Culture*, Strategic Studies Institute Monograph (Carlisle, PA: US Army War College, 2002), p. 19. It is available at http://www.carlisle.army.mil/ssi/pdffiles/PUB60.pdf.
47. 'Chinese media sees red,' Press Trust of India, 3 March 2006.
48. Ashley J. Tellis, 'The China-Pakistan Nuclear Deal: Separating Fact From Fiction,' Carnegie Endowment for International Peace, 16 July 2010, available at http://carnegieendowment.org/files/china pak nuke1.pdf.

49. R. Jeffry Smith and Joby Warrick, 'A Nuclear Power's Act of Proliferation,' *Washington Post*, 13 November 2009.
50. For a detailed explication of the Chinese nuclear posture vis-à-vis India, see Pravin Sawhney, *The Defence Makeover: 10 Myths that Shape India's Image* (New Delhi: Sage Publications, 2003).
51. Bharat Karnad, *Nuclear Weapons and Indian Security* (New Delhi: Macmillan India Ltd., 2002), p. xix.
52. Larry Wortzel, *China's Nuclear Forces: Operations, Training, Doctrine, Command, Control and Campaign Planning*, Strategic Studies Institute Monograph (Carlislie, PA: US Army War College 2007). It is available at www.strategicstudiesinstitute.army.mil/pdffiles/pub776.pdf.
53. Jing-dong Yuan, 'Chinese Perceptions of the Utility of Nuclear Weapons: Problems and Potential Problems in Disarmament,' Proliferation Papers. No. 34, Spring 2010.
54. 'Separate J-K visa row: India conveys "concern" to China,' *Indian Express*, New Delhi, 2 October 2009.
55. Shishir Gupta, 'Hindi-China, by and by,' *Indian Express*, New Delhi, 11 January 2008.
56. Shishir Gupta, 'Tibet gets connected, Delhi gets reminder: what about our roads?' *Indian Express*, New Delhi, 30 August 2004.
57. C. Raja Mohan, 'Importance of being Dalai Lama,' *Indian Express*, New Delhi, 14 March 2005.
58. Anil K. Joseph, 'China unimpressed by Dalai's overtures,' Press Trust of India, 11 March 2005.
59. Andrew Jacobs, 'Tibetans Fear a Broader Crackdown,' *New York Times*, 23 June 2010.
60. Arun Shourie, *Art of War*, New Delhi: Rupa, 2008.
61. Pallavi Singh, 'Govt asks ministers to skip Dalai Lama

function, meanwhile HRD will fund one,' *Indian Express*, New Delhi, 6 November 2007.
62. Saurabh Shukla, 'Beijing Games,' *India Today*, 13 June 2008.
63. Pranab Dhal Samanta, 'China raises Sikkim boundary dispute during Pranab visit,' *Indian Express*, New Delhi, 8 June 2008.
64. Saurabh Shukla, 'Creeping Aggression,' *India Today*, 15 October 2007.
65. 'Need to develop areas bordering China,' *Indian Express*, New Delhi, 2 December 2007.
66. Raghvendra Rao, 'If Govt can't deliver, allow us to go to China for rail line: Arunachal MP,' *Indian Express*, New Delhi, 11 March 2008.
67. Bhavna Vij-Aurora, 'Gangtok Junction,' *Outlook*, 28 August 2007.
68. 'Pranab admits Chinese incursions, but says no need to panic,' *Indian Express*, New Delhi, 13 January 2008.
69. 'India has lost "substantial" land to China: Official Report,' Press Trust of India, 10 January 2010.
70. 'PM cools hot air over China,' *Indian Express*, New Delhi, 19 September 2009.

4. A Contrast in Global Profiles

1. For the seminal exposition of the reasons behind the rise and subsequent decline of great powers, see Paul Kennedy, *The Rise and Fall of the Great Powers: Economic Change and Military Conflict from 1500 to 2000* (New York: Random House, 1987).
2. This argument is made in detail in Michael D. Swaine and Ashley J. Tellis, *Interpreting China's Grand Strategy: Past, Present and Future* (Santa Monica, CA: Rand Corp., 2000).

3. Raphael Israeli, 'The People's Republic of China and the PLO,' in Norton and Greenberg, *The International Relations of the PLO* (Carbondale, IL, 1989).
4. Alan Hutchinson, *China's Africa Revolution* (London: Hutchinson & Co, 1975).
5. On 'soft balancing', see Robert A. Pape, 'Soft Balancing Against the United States,' *International Security*, Vol. 30, No. 1 (Summer 2005), pp. 7-45.
6. On China's use of 'soft power', see Joshua Kurlantzick, *Charm Offensive: How China's Soft Power Is Transforming the World* (New Haven, CT: Yale University Press, 2007).
7. For two of the most powerful articulations of this view, see Kishore Mahbubani, *The New Asian Hemisphere: The Irresistible Shift of Global Power to the East* (New York: Public Affairs, 2008); and Fareed Zakaria, *The Post-American World* (New York: W.W. Norton & Co, 2008).
8. The term 'post-American' has been used by Fareed Zakaria to describe his conception of the emerging global order.
9. For a discussion of the various interpretations of China's 'peaceful rise,' see Evan S. Medeiros, 'China Debates Its "Peaceful Rise" Strategy?' available at http://yaleglobal.yale.edu/display.article?id=4118.
10. For an assessment of the great power potential of China, India and Japan in the 1980s, see Stephen Cohen, 'Toward a Great State in Asia?' in Onkar Marwah and Jonathan D. Pollack (eds) *Military Power and Policy in Asian States: China, India, and Japan* (Boulder, CO: Westview, 1980), pp. 9-41.
11. Bill Emmott, *Rivals: How the Power Struggle Between China, India and Japan Will Shape Our Next Decade* (London, Allen Lane, 2008), pp. 1-24.

12. On the role of nationalism in the shaping of Japan-China ties, see Yutaka Kawashima, *Japanese Foreign Policy at the Crossroads* (Washington, DC: Brookings Institution Press, 2003, pp. 104-106.
13. Robert Marquand, 'Anti-Japan protests jar an uneasy Asia,' *Christian Science Monitor*, 11 April 2005.
14. 'Asian row turns to wartime past,' *BBC*, 19 April 2005, http://news.bbc.co.uk/1/hi/world/asia-pacific/4459243.stm.
15. Ashley Tellis, 'India in Asian Geopolitics,' in Prakash Nanda (ed.), *Rising India: Friends and Foes* (New Delhi: Lancer Publishers, 2007), pp. 123-127.
16. John Pomfret, 'US sells weapons to Taiwan, angering China,' *Washington Post*, 30 January 2010.
17. John Pomfret, 'Beijing claims "indisputable sovereignty" over South China Sea,' *Washington Post*, 31 July 2010.
18. The statistics on China's oil consumption vis-à-vis the world are available at http://www.xist.org/charts/en_oilcons.aspx.
19. The Chinese Government's White Paper on Africa released in 2006 is available at http://news.xinhuanet.com/english/2006-01/12/content_4042521.htm.
20. I. Taylor, 'Taiwan's Foreign Policy and Africa: The Limitations of Dollar Diplomacy,' *Journal of Contemporary China II*, 30, pp. 125-40.
21. 'China-Africa trade hits US$55.5 billion in 2006,' *People's Daily*, 30 January 2007.
22. Sahil Mahatani, 'The Rise of Sino-African Relations,' *Far Eastern Economic Review*, 7 October 2008.
23. 'Summit adopts declaration, action plan,' *China Daily*, 5 November 2006.
24. On China's recent reliance on its soft power in its

dealings with other states, see Kurlantzick, *Charm Offensive* (New Haven, CT: Yale University Press, 2007).

25. Denis M. Tull, 'China's Engagement in Africa: Scope, Significance and Consequences,' *Journal of Modern African Studies*, Vol. 44, No. 3 (2006), pp. 459-79.

26. Yaroslav Trofimov, 'In Africa, China's expansion begins to stir resentment,' *Wall Street Journal*, 2 February 2007.

27. The National Security Strategy of the United States of America, The White House, March 2006, available at http://www.whitehouse.gov/nsc/nss/2006/nss2006.pdf.

28. Dan Blumenthal, '*Providing Arms: China and the Middle East,*' *Middle East Quarterly*, Spring 2005, pp. 11-9.

29. Leila Fadel and Ernesto Londono, 'Risk-tolerant China investing heavily in Iraq as US companies hold back,' *Washington Post*, 2 July 2010.

30. Jonathan Rynhold and Deng-Ker Lee, 'Peking's Middle East Policy in Post Cold War Era,' *Issues and Studies*, Vol. 30, No. 8 (August 1994), p. 85.

31. 'The Worldwide Threat: Evolving Dangers in a Complex World,' Testimony of Director of Central Intelligence, George J. Tenet, before the Senate Select Committee on Intelligence, 11 February 2003. Available at <http://www.cia.gov/cia/public_affairs/speeches/dci_ speech_02112003.html>.

32. Tyler Bridges, 'China makes big moves in Latin America,' *The Miami Herald*, 8 October 2009.

33. Alexei Barrionuevo, 'To fortify China, soybean harvest grows in Brazil,' *New York Times*, 6 April 2007.

34. For a detailed analysis of Sino-Russian defence relationship and its implications for the U.S. foreign policy, see Alexander V. Nemets and John L. Scherer, 'The Emerging Sino-Russian Axis,' *The World & I*, Vol. 15, no. 6 (June 2000): 72.

35. Andrew C. Kuchins, 'Limits of the Sino-Russian Strategic Partnership,' in *Russia After the Fall*, Andrew C. Kuchins ed., 212. (Washington, DC: Carnegie Endowment for International Peace, 2002).
36. 'Trade between China, Russia on Upward Trend,' http://ce.cei/gov/cn/enew/new_e2/e41d0g58.htm.
37. 'China's Security Stance,' *Jane's Defence Weekly*, 18 December 2002.
38. Vladimir Radyuhin, 'Shanghai group denounces misuse of anti-terror war,' *Hindu*, Chennai, 30 May 2003.
39. Stephen Blank, 'China quietly reshapes Asia,' Jamestown Foundation, 12 August 2009.
40. For an example of how smaller South Asian states have used China as a leverage in their dealings with India, see Manish Dabhade and Harsh V. Pant, 'Coping with Challenges to Sovereignty: Sino-Indian Rivalry and Nepal's Foreign Policy,' *Contemporary South Asia*, Vol. 13, No. 2 (June 2004), pp. 157-169.
41. Ananth Krishnan, 'China's fighter jets for Pakistan,' *Hindu*, Chennai, 11 November 2009.
42. Tarique Niazi, 'China's March on South Asia,' *China Brief*, Vol. 5. No. 9, 26 April 2005.
43. Pranab Dhal Samanta, 'Pro-China centres, calling for reduced ties with Delhi, sprout along Nepal border with India,' *Indian Express*, New Delhi, 11 February 2008.
44. Ashok K. Mehta, 'Colombo looks beyond Delhi,' *Pioneer*, 18 March 2009.
45. Seema Sirohi, 'Africa Investment,' *Outlook*, 6 April 2008.
46. Liz Mathew, 'Africa's needs are great enough for both India and China: Tharoor,' *Mint*, New Delhi, 8 February 2010.
47. Bill Gertz, 'China builds up strategic sea lanes,' *Washington Times*, 18 January 2005.

48. C. Raja Mohan, 'The battle for Africa,' *Indian Express*, New Delhi, 10 May 2006.
49. Sudha Ramachandran, 'Myanmar plays off India and China,' *Asia Times*, 17 August 2005, available at http://www.atimes.com/atimes/South_Asia/GH17Df01.html.
50. 'Natural gas export: Yangon chooses China,' *Hindu*, Chennai, 22 March 2007.
51. Stephen J. Blank, *U.S. Interests in Central Asia and the Challenges to Them*, Testimony to the Subcommittee on the Middle East and Central Asia, House Committee on International Relations, 25 July 2006, available at http://www.internationalrelations.house.gov/archives/109/bla072506.pdf.
52. M. Li Nan, 'The Role of the Military in Guaranteeing Access,' Joint Energy Security Programme, RUSI—Westminster Energy Forum, 1–2 December 2005.
53. C. Le Miere, *Gunboat Diplomacy in Maritime Energy Disputes*. Joint Energy Security Programme, RUSI—Westminster Energy Forum, 1–2 December 2005.
54. P. Keun-Wook, 'Geopolitics of Pipeline Development in NE Asia: Implications for China's Natural Gas Expansion,' Joint Energy Security Programme, RUSI—Westminster Energy Forum, 1–2 December 2005.
55. J. Nandakumar, 'China and our energy,' *Financial Express*, New Delhi, 6 April 2006.
56. Vladimir Radyuhin, 'Lessons for India as Russia ups ante,' *Hindu*, Chennai, 2 January 2007.
57. T.S.G. Rethinaraj, 'China's Energy and Regional Security Perspectives,' *Defense & Security Analysis*, Vol. 19, no. 4 (2003): 382.
58. Ibid., 383.
59. Matthew Wheeler, 'China expands its southern sphere of influence,' *Jane's Intelligence Review* 17, no. 6 (June 2005): 42.

60. Chietigj Bajpaee, 'Energy Fuels Cold War,' *Asia Times*, 2 March 2005, available at www.atimes.com/atimes/China/GC02Ad07.html.
61. Gal Luft, 'Fuelling the Dragon: China's race into the oil market,' *Institute for the Analysis of Global Security*, available at http://www.iags.org/china.htm.
62. Walter Russell Mead, 'Why we're in the Gulf,' *Wall Street Journal*, 27 December 2007.
63. J. Roberts, 'New Areas for Competition and Co-operation: Caspian and Middle East Enticements,' Joint Energy Security Programme, RUSI—Westminster Energy Forum, 1–2 December 2005.
64. A. Zwaniecki, 'U.S.-China Cooperation Could Advance Mutual, Global Energy Goals,' http://usinfo.state.gov/eap/Archive/2005/Apr/04-622583.html.
65. Indrajit Basu, 'India discreet, China bold in oil hunt.' *Asia Times*, 29 September 2005, available at http://www.atimes.com/atimes/South_Asia/GI29Df01.html
66. D. Thompson, 'China's Global Strategy for Energy, Security and Diplomacy,' The Jamestown Foundation, *China Brief*, Vol. 5, No. 7, 2005, p. 2
67. 'China, India fight for African oil,' Associated Foreign Press, 15 October 2004.
68. Gordon Smith, 'Indian and Chinese oil group agree deal,' *Financial Times*, 20 December 2005.
69. Rakateem Katakey and John Duce, 'India loses to China in Africa-to-Kazakhstan-to-Venezuela oil,' *Bloomberg News*, 29 June 2010.
70. 'India, China will flirt, not wed, in foreign oil push,' Reuters, 21 December 2005.
71. James Traub, 'The world according to China,' *New York Times*, 3 September 2006.

5. INDIA'S CHINA PROBLEM: WHY THE LACK OF A SERIOUS RESPONSE

1. 'Pleasing Beijing, govt tells its ministers don't attend Dalai Lama honour function,' *Indian Express*, New Delhi, 4 November 2007.
2. Somini Sengupta, 'India tiptoes in China's footsteps to compete but not offend,' *New York Times*, 4 April 2008.
3. This definition is borrowed from Ronald Jepperson, Alexander Wendt and Peter Katzenstein, 'Norms, Identity, and Culture in National Security,' in Peter Katzenstein (ed.), *The Culture of National Security: Norms and Identity in World Politics* (New York: Columbia University Press, 1996), p. 56.
4. Ibid p. 32.
5. For the sources of Chinese realpolitik strategic culture, see Alastair Iain Johnston, 'Cultural Realism and Strategy in Maoist China,' in Jepperson et al., *The Culture of National Security*, pp. 216-268.
6. Alastair Iain Johnston, *Cultural Realism: Strategic Culture and Grand Strategy in Chinese History* (Princeton, NJ: Princeton University Press, 1995).
7. Andrew Scobell, *China and Strategic Culture*, Strategic Studies Institute Monograph (Carlisle, PA: US Army War College, 2002), pp. 14-20. It is available at http://www.carlislie.army.mil/ssi/pdffiles/PUB60.pdf.
8. Srinjoy Chowdhury, 'India "a Hitler in a Dhoti"?' *Statesman*, Kolkata, 29 November 2004.
9. George Tanham, *Indian Strategic Thought: An Interpretive Essay* (Santa Monica, CA: RAND Corp., 1992).
10. Jaswant Singh, *Defending India* (New York: St. Martin's Press, 1999), pp. 1-58.

11. Ibid., p. 34.
12. For details, see the Election Manifesto of the National Democratic Alliance led by the BJP for the 1999 parliamentary elections at http://www.bjp.org.
13. Ashley J. Tellis, *India's Emerging Nuclear Posture: Between Recessed Deterrent and Ready Arsenal* (New York: Oxford University Press, 2001), p. 658.
14. On the problems confronting the Indian higher education system, see Devesh Kapur and Pratap Bhanu Mehta, 'Indian Higher Education Reform: From Half-Baked Socialism to Half-Baked Capitalism,' Working Paper No. 108, Center for International Development, Harvard University, available at http://www.cid.harvard.edu/cidwp/pdf/108.pdf.
15. The seminal text on structural-realist theory in international relations remains Kenneth N. Waltz, *Theory of International Politics* (Reading: Addison-Wesley, 1979).
16. 'All Parties for "Purposeful" Relations with China,' Press Trust of India, 8 September 2004.
17. This typology of India's China Debate has been borrowed from Mohan Malik, *Eyeing the Dragon: India's China Debate*, Asia Pacific Center for Security Studies, Honolulu, December 2003, available at http://www.apcss.org/Publications/SAS/ ChinaDebate/ChinaDebate_Malik.pdf.
18. Steven A, Hoffman, 'Perception and China Policy in India,' in Francine Frankel and Harry Harding (eds), *The India-China Relationship: What the United States Needs to Know*, pp. 39-49.
19. 'PM pulls up Jairam Ramesh for Beijing blunder,' *Times of India*, New Delhi, 11 May 2010.
20. For economic indicators, see The World Bank, World

Development Indicators Database, July 2008, at http://www.worldbank.org/data/databytopic/GDP_PPP.pdf. The latest figures on military capabilities can be found in International Institute for Strategic Studies (IISS), The Military Balance 2008-09 (London: IISS, 2008).
21. Hans J. Morgenthau, 'Vietnam: Shadow and Substance,' *New York Review of Books*, 16 September 1965.
22. The full transcript of this speech is available at http://www.iiss.org.uk/conferences/iiss-citi-india-global-forum/igf-plenary-sessions-2008/opening-remarks-and-dinner-address/dinner-address-kamal-nath.
23. Michael Sheehan, *The Balance of Power: History and Theory* (London: Routledge, 1996), p. 7.
24. K. Subrahmanyam, *Indian Security Perspectives* (New Delhi: ABC Publishing House, 1982), p. 127.
25. Ibid., p. 129.
26. This point has been eloquently elaborated in Ashley J. Tellis, 'Future Fire: Challenges Facing Indian Defence Policy in the New Century,' delivered at the India Today Conclave, New Delhi, 13 March 2004, available at http://www.ceip.org/files/pdf/futurefire.pdf.
27. Quoted in P.V.R. Rao, *India's Defence Policy and Organisation Since Independence* (New Delhi: The United Services Institution of India, 1977), pp. 5-6.
28. This argument has been explicated in Philip Bobbitt, *The Shield of Achilles: War, Peace, and the Course of History* (New York: Anchor Books, 2003).
29. Robert Art, 'To What Ends Military Power,' *International Security*, Vol. 4 (Spring 1980), pp. 4-35.
30. K. Subrahmanyam, *Perspectives in Defence Planning* (New Delhi: Abhinav, 1972), pp. 126-133.
31. Lorne J. Kavic, *India's Quest for Security: Defence Policies, 1947-1965* (Berkeley: University of California Press, 1967), p. 192.

32. Tellis, *Future Fire*.
33. Scobell, *China and Strategic Culture*, pp. 4–10.
34. Shaun Randol, 'How to Approach the Elephant: Chinese Perceptions of India in the Twenty-First Century,' *Asian Affairs: An American Review*, June 2008, pp. 211–226.
35. Susan Shirk, 'One-Sided Rivalry: China's Perceptions and Policies Toward India,' in Francine Frankel and Harry Harding (eds) *The India-China Relationship*.
36. Shekhar Gupta, 'A hotline to Burkina Faso?' *Indian Express*, New Delhi, 26 January 2004.
37. A sense of the thinking of the Indian communist parties on foreign policy can be found in Harkishen Singh Surjeet, 'On foreign policy, UPA has been clever by half,' *Indian Express*, New Delhi, 18 April 2005. For a trenchant critique of the stance of the communist parties on many issues of Indian national security, see G. Parthasarthy, 'Left's Unkindly Cut,' *Tribune*, Chandigarh, 10 March 2005.
38. The prime minister's speech at the India Today Conclave delivered on 25 February 2005 is available at http://pmindia.nic.in/speeches.htm.
39. See, for example, C. Raja Mohan, 'India and China: A shifting paradigm,' *Hindu*, Chennai, 29 July 2004.
40. K. Subrahmanyam, 'China discovers multipolarity,' *Tribune*, Chandigarh, 13 April 2005.
41. Jairam Ramesh, *Making Sense of ChindiA: Reflections on China and India* (New Delhi: India Research Press, 2005).
42. See, for example, 'Settling India, China border dispute will take time: Krishna,' Press Trust of India, 7 April 2010.
43. Ananth Krishnan, 'Relations with China not externally driven: India.' *Hindu*, Chennai, 7 July 2010.

44. 'Rise of China New security challenge to India: Pranab,' *Indian Express*, New Delhi, 4 November 2008.
45. 'No Chinese military bases in the Indian Ocean, says Menon,' *Indian Express*, New Delhi, 11 September 2009.
46. 'China keeps India out,' Press Trust of India, 29 March 2008.

Epilogue

1. 'China plans to slow expansion of defense spending in 2010,' *Washington Post*, 5 March 2010.
2. Shen Dingli, 'Don't shun the idea of setting up military bases overseas,' 28 January 2010, available at http://www.china.org.cn/opinion/2010-01-28/content_19324522.htm.
3. Frank Ching, 'China's military objectives reach far beyond Taiwan,' *China Post*, 12 May 2010.
4. Saibal Dasgupta, 'China mulls setting up military base in Pakistan,' *Times of India*, New Delhi, 28 January 2010.

INDEX

Africa and China relations, 84–90
agriculture sector, 20, 24
Aiyar, Mani Shankar, 31–32
Aksai Plain, Chinese occupation, 11
Al Furat Production Company, 32
Andaman Sea, 109
anti-dumping measures, 20, 45
Arabian Sea, 57
Aramco Overseas Company, 114–15
armed forces, modernization, China, 53, 92
Arunachal Pradesh, Chinese intrusion, 2, 3, 7, 63, 69, 70
Asian Development Bank (ADB), 2, 69
Asia-Pacific
  Indian policy, 147
  shifting centre of gravity, 76–84
Association of South East Asian Nations (ASEAN), 5–6, 83
authoritarianism, China, 39, 74, 113

Bangladesh and China relations, 100, 102, 107
Bay of Bengal, 55, 109
  Chinese presence, 57
Beijing Gas Group Company, 32
Bhabha Atomic Research Centre (BARC), 50
Bhagat, P.S., 150
Bharatiya Janata Party (BJP), 126, 143
Bhutan, Chinese intrusions into, 68–69
Bobbitt, Philip, 136
border issue/dispute, 33, 64–71
  Chinese infrastructure development, 2, 7
  Chinese intrusion, 11, 16–19, 52, 114

INDEX

Indian policy, 1, 3, 9, 52
Border Roads Organization (BRO), 108
Brazil and China ties, 97–98
British Petroleum (BP), 118
Brooks, Henderson, 150
bunker system, 56
Bush, George W., 79

Cambodia, 113
carbon emission caps, 20, 21
Caspian Sea, 110
Central Asian oil politics, 110
Central Intelligence Agency (CIA), 10
Chashma III & IV, 60
China
    Africa Summit, 106
    ASEAN Free Trade Agreement, 83
    Chinese Communist Party (CCP), 38–40, 140
    Chinese Nationalist Party, 151
    direct investment in Africa, 86
    emerging superpower, 4, 42, 72, 133, 138, 156
    expansionism, 49, 69, 115, 154, 156, 157
    Metallurgical Group, 106
    minimum nuclear doctrine, 62
    National Climate Programme, 23
    National Nuclear Cooperation, 60
    National Petroleum Corporation (CNPC), 111, 117
    strategy of containing India, 100
    Study Centres (CSCs), 103
Chittagong port, 102
Churchill, Winston, 153
climate change, India and China coordinated efforts, 19, 20–23
Cold War, 73, 85, 98, 102, 130
communism, 40
Communist Party of India-Marxists (CPM), 132
compressed natural gas (CNG), 32
Congress, 121, 17
conventional war-fighting doctrine, 51
corruption, 87, 89
cultural and educational exchange, 33
cultural attractiveness, China, 75
cultural differences, 41
cyber and space warfare technologies, China, 49, 50

Dalai Lama, 50, 63, 68, 120–21
    government-in-exile, 65–67
declarations abound, 16–18
defence expenditure, China, 47–48
defence issues, India, 125, 137
    planning and force structuring, 148

democratic institutional structure, Indian, 41, 43
democratic reforms, China, 40
Deng Xiaoping, 38, 76, 155
diplomatic outreach, China, 75, 131
Dixit, J.N., 17
Doha negotiations, 23
domestic political constraints, India, 9
domestic politics, India, 135

East Asia
  Free Trade Area, 6
  security architecture, 83
East China Sea, 156
  economic and military capabilities, India, 133
economic
  trajectory, China, 19, 34, 38–40, 42–46, 72–74, 90, 113
  India, 19, 134, 138
  integration, China and India, 18, 34, 142
  globalization, 92
  interdependence in South Asia, 149
electronic warfare, 50
energy matrix, energy security, 24–33
  demand-supply gap, 28
  India, 115
  India's loss is China's gain, 115–19
  Sino-Indian cooperation, 107

environmental degradation, 89
ethnic movements, 18, 99, 133
European Coal and Steel Community, 32
European Union (EU), 24
Exxon Mobil Corporation, 118

Fernandes, George, 139
financial crisis (2008–09), 19, 41–44, 76
Finger Area, 64
food security and livelihood issues, 24
foreign direct investment (FDI), China, 42, 45, 75
foreign policy
  China, 2, 28, 42, 72, 74, 124
  India, 11, 12, 28, 37, 121–25, 133, 135–36, 138–43, 152
  making process, institutionalization, 126–30, 137, 148
  United States, 79
Free Trade Agreement (FTA), 106
fuel efficiency cap, 23

G-2 (global condominium of US and China), 79–80
Gandhi, Sonia, 120
Gas Authority of India Limited (GAIL), 32
geopolitical interests, China, 72
GhostNet, 50
GPS-blocking technology, 53

INDEX

greenhouse gas emissions, 22
Guangzhou, 115
Gulf Cooperation Council (GCC), 106
Gulf War, 1991, 46
Gwadar port, Pakistan, 55, 57, 102

Hainan Island, 54–55
Hambantota Development Zone, 56
Hindu view of life, 125
Hoffman, Steven, 131
Hormuz Strait, 57
Hu Jintao, 38
Hussein, Saddam, 19, 92

India and China
  bilateral relations, 1–2, 17, 33–36, 37, 41–42, 44, 85, 99–106, 139, 142, 147
  energy cooperation, 107
  Free Trade Agreement (FTA), 45
  global partnership, 144–45
  growing challenges, 4–6
  agreement on peace and tranquility (1993), 68
  strategic rivalry, 5, 130–33
  war (1962), 1, 4, 10, 138, 150
  China policy, 123–25
  China-Is-Hostile position, 131
  China-Is-Not-Hostile perspective, 131
  Chinese intrusions, 3, 68, 69
global
  coordination and bilateral tensions, 2–4, 74
  economy, 19, 20, 44, 46, 77, 141
  energy resources, Sino-Indian competition, 7
  financial networks, 20
  inter-state hierarchy, 36
  peace and stability, 77
  politics, 6, 12, 13, 33, 77, 123, 130, 134, 136, 138, 140, 146
  power balance, 4
  profiles, China and India, contrast, 71, 72ff
  structural imperative, 18–20
  trade dynamic, 20, 23–24
India-Iran gas pipeline, 32
Indian Navy, 53
Indian Ocean, Chinese strategic presence, 3, 53–58, 100, 109, 146, 156
industrialization, 28
infrastructure upgradation, Coco Islands, 55–56
intellectual divide, 121–22
international community, 65, 67, 92, 101
International Monetary Fund (IMF), 82, 87
international system, 121, 130, 133, 135–37
Iran, 95, 113

China, energy relations, 92–95, 97, 111–15, 117
nuclear issues, 82
Iraq, United States' invasion, 19, 92, 115
Islamic fundamentalism/insurgency, 18, 26, 95, 99, 109
in Kashmir, 102
in Xinjiang, 102
Israel and China energy relations, 93, 97

Jairam Ramesh, 132, 142
Japan
and China trade relations, 78, 79
and United States, dispute, 83
Jiang Zemin, 38, 93
Joint Working Group (JWG), 16–17, 63

Kamal Nath, 134
Kargil conflict, 35
Kashmir, 63, 80
Khan, Abdul Qadeer, 61
Kissinger, Henry, 143
Korea, North, 113
nuclear issues, 82

land-based ballistic missiles, 62
Liao Shao Chi, 10
Line of Actual Control (LAC), 3, 16, 63, 64, 68, 70

Line of Control, 63
Look East policy, 5, 88

Mahmud al-Zahar, 93
Malacca Strait, 54, 56, 109, 111
maritime space and resources, China, 53, 156
Mbeki, Thabo, 90
McMahon line, 63
Menon, Shiv Shankar, 144–45
Middle East and China energy relations, 90–97, 110, 107
military modernization, military power
China, 8, 46–52, 93
India, 136–37
Japan, 78
Mugabe, Robert G., 88
Mukherjee, Pranab, 70, 145
multiculturalism, 143
Multi-party democracy, 38
Mumbai, terrorist attack (26 November 2008), 3
Myanmar and China relations, 107–09, 113

Nanjing, Japanese occupation, 78
Nathu La pass, 17, 70
national security matrix, 136
nationalism as an ideology, 41
naval expansion, China, 53–58
Nehru, Jawaharlal, 10, 11, 41, 121, 125, 136, 137
Nepal and China relations, 100, 102, 103, 104

nuclear dimension, 8, 26, 58–62, 94
  confidence building and risk reduction measures, 58–59
  doctrine for China, India, and Pakistan, 58
  no-first-use policy, 62
Nuclear Non-Proliferation Treaty (NPT), 58–59
Nuclear Suppliers Group (NSG), 3, 59, 60–61
nuclear test, India (1998), 15

OAO Udmurtneft fields, 112
Obama, Barack, 2, 21, 76, 79
Oil and Natural Gas Corporation (ONGC), 111, 118
oil exploration in Indian Ocean, 107
oil prices, 27, 28
oil security, 113
Olympics, Beijing, 2008, 39
ONGC Videsh Ltd (OVL), 112
Organization of Petroleum Exporting Countries (OPEC), 115

Pakistan
  China relations, 35, 61, 80, 157
  nuclear aid, 61, 100, 102, 105
  India relation/security concern, 4, 5, 36, 105, 143–44, 157
Pakistan-occupied Kashmir, 102

Palestinians, 93
Panchen Lama, 66
Panchsheel, 11
People's Liberation Army (PLA), 45, 54, 66, 82
People's Liberation Army Navy (PLAN), 53, 156
Petro Canada, 32
Petro Kazakhstan, 111
Planning Commission, Integrated Energy Policy Report, 29
political trajectory, China, 38–42
power politics, 12, 14, 135
purchasing power parity, 28, 133

Rajpaksa, Mahinda, 104
Rao, Nirupama, 42
Revolution in Military Affairs (RMA), China, 46–47
Rosneft, 112
Royal Dutch Shell, 32, 118
Rudd, Kevin, 80
Russia and China, relations, 98–99

Sakhalin-I, 112
Saudi Arabia and China energy relations, 95, 114
security dilemma, India, 6–8
Shanghai Cooperation Organization (SCO), 99, 110
ship-building infrastructure, China, 57
Sikkim border issue, 3, 17, 68, 69

Siliguri corridor, 69
Singh, Jaswant, 125
Singh, Manmohan, 18, 64, 139–40
Singh, Natwar, 58
Sino. *See* China
Sittwe Port, 108
South Asia and China, 99–106
South Asian Association for Regional Cooperation (SAARC), 104–05
South China Sea, 54, 55, 84
Soviet Union, disintegration, 40, 130
space weaponization, China, 50
string of pearls strategy, China, 55, 107
Sri Lanka
  China relations, 100, 102, 103, 104
  India political and economic influences, 103
  socio-economic development, 105
Stern, Todd, 81
strategic planning architecture, India, 74, 125, 130, 156
Strategic Policy Group, 127
Sun Tzu, 154
Syria and China relation, 93, 94, 117

Taiwan, 75, 76, 81, 83; 85
Taliban, 80
Tanham, George, 125
Tawang, 63, 64
technology, Sino-Indian cooperation, 34–35
territorial disputes/issues, 63–71, 124, 156
terrorism, Sino-Indian cooperation on combating, 18, 35, 99, 113
Tibet
  Chinese sovereignty, 17, 76, 83, 103, 121, 151 Chinese military use, 65–70
  riots (2008), 67, 70
TNK-BP, 112
trade deficit, 44
trade relations, 33–34
trade surplus, China, 75

Uighur insurgency, 96
United Nations (UN), 19, 20, 58, 75, 94, 108, 116
  Human Rights Council, 108
  peacekeeping efforts, 51
  General Assembly, 155
  Security Council, 5, 92, 94, 109, 118, 133, 151–52
United Progressive Alliance (UPA), 127
urbanization, 25
United States of America
  and Afghanistan war, 46
  China relations, 6, 79–80, 94, 97–99, 141;
  economic dependence on, 3
  dependence on the Middle East, 114

domestic climate change, 21
India civilian nuclear energy cooperation pact, 3, 7, 13, 59–62, 121
Indian maritime cooperation in the Indian Ocean, 57
international dominance, 18–19, 21, 77, 91, 119
Iraq war, 19, 46, 99
Japan relationship, 80, 83
military vulnerabilities, 49
National Intelligence Council, 101
naval activity in the Persian Gulf, 57
power decline, 90–91, 147
terrorist attack (9/11/2001), 99
war on terror, 84, 114
Yugoslavia, war, 19

Vajpayee, Atal Bihari, 16, 139
Vietnam, 113

weapons of mass destruction (WMD) (or v/v), 94
Wen Jiabao, 33, 64
World Bank, 87
World Economic Forum, 81–82
World Trade Organization (WTO), 20, 45
World War, Second, 76, 79, 83

Xinjiang Autonomous Region, 52, 96, 102, 111

Yadavaran, 117
Yugoslavia, US campaign, 19

Zhu Rongji, 34

ABOUT THE AUTHOR

Harsh V. Pant teaches at King's College, London, in the Department of Defence Studies. He is also an Associate with the King's Centre for Science and Security Studies and an Affiliate with the King's India Institute. His current research is focused on Asia-Pacific security and defence issues. His most recent books include *Contemporary Debates in Indian Foreign and Security Policy* (Palgrave Macmillan) and *Indian Foreign Policy in a Unipolar World* (Routledge).